RIVERS WANTED

Does God Still Speak Today?
Extraordinary Dreams And Visions
From God To Encourage Your Life

Rivers Teske

WESTBOW
PRESS®
A DIVISION OF THOMAS NELSON
& ZONDERVAN

This book is a work of non-fiction. Unless otherwise noted, the author
and the publisher make no explicit guarantees as to the accuracy of
the information contained in this book and in some cases, names
of people and places have been altered to protect their privacy.

WestBow Press books may be ordered through
booksellers or by contacting:

WestBow Press
A Division of Thomas Nelson & Zondervan
1663 Liberty Drive
Bloomington, IN 47403
www.westbowpress.com
1 (866) 928-1240

Scriptures taken from the Holy Bible, New International Version®, NIV®.
Copyright © 1973, 1978, 1984, 2011 by Biblica, Inc.™ Used by permission
of Zondervan. All rights reserved worldwide. www.zondervan.com
The "NIV" and "New International Version" are trademarks registered
in the United States Patent and Trademark Office by Biblica, Inc.™

ISBN: 978-1-9736-7831-1 (sc)
ISBN: 978-1-9736-7832-8 (hc)
ISBN: 978-1-9736-7830-4 (e)

Library of Congress Control Number: 2019916988

Print information available on the last page.

WestBow Press rev. date: 12/26/2019

I dedicate this book to

God, who invaded my life,

Paul, my beloved husband and spiritual companion,

My children, Tara, Paul II, and Jordan: I love you deeply and forever,

My grandchildren: Tyler, Olivia, and Jackson, my legacy. May you dream dreams and serve the Lord all the days of your life, and

My friends who encouraged me and pushed me to finish this book.

Contents

Contents

Introduction

Have you ever been at a place in your life where you were confused and did not know what to do? In the midst of that uncertainty, did you ask God to give you a sign for confirmation? If He responded with a sign, was it subtle, or did He rock your world with more than you bargained for? If these questions resonate in your life, then this book is for you. *Rivers Wanted* is a book about a mainline pastor's wife and her struggle to understand the power of the Holy Spirit, which turned life upside down through a supernatural personal encounter. In her desperate search for faith, the meaning of life, and the Father's love, she would eventually come face to face with her greatest fears: Could she really trust God? Was there a God who cared and wanted her? Did God even exist? In a quest for the answers to these questions, a dramatic and specific sign from Him, coupled with astonishing dreams and visions, subsequently changed her life after twenty-three years in ministry. She received more than she ever imagined by asking a simple request from the God she had lost hope and faith in. It is a remarkable story of how God wove Himself into the very fabric of her life.

Sprinkled throughout you will find her journey relatable and heartfelt as she shares the extraordinary measures God used to help her overcome the inner battles she faced. Like all of us, she would have to find her voice again.

In learning to hear and trust God's voice, there were three critical things the process taught her. First, that God not only speaks to His people through His Holy Word, but surprisingly, He also communicates in a variety of ways, audible and inaudible, to our ears and hearts, in dreams and visions, and through messengers, human or angelic.

Second, she learned to identify how God was teaching her to persevere through endurance with the reassurance that He was there through all her battles. This took practice; it took solitude, at times, and a passionate pursuit of God to meet her deepest needs. To hear the still quiet voice that engaged her over time also took patience in studying the Word of God. In the final analysis, all these elements would shape her life for the destiny God was calling her to.

Third, she found that when God speaks, it is truth. Jesus says, "And I will ask the Father, and he will give you another Counselor to be with you forever ... the Spirit of truth. The world cannot accept him, because it neither sees him nor knows him, but you know him, for he lies with you and will be in you" (John 14:16–17). He will never violate or contradict His sacred word or His character and nature. She discovered that the rational mind was a great gift from God, but too often, the mind justifies the desires of the flesh and rationalizes what an individual wants to do, even if it contradicts His Word. Her first litmus test when hearing the messages from God was to measure it against scripture.

Lastly, she found that God takes His people through incredible situations (sometimes almost unbearable) so that on the other side, they can minister to people going through similar experiences. The apostle Paul spells it out beautifully: "Praise be to the God and Father of our Lord Jesus Christ, the Father of compassion and the God all comfort, who comforts us in all our troubles, so that we can comfort those in any trouble with the comfort we ourselves have received from God" (2 Corinthians 1:3–4). You will be encouraged in her story to see how God answered her prayers to give hope, purpose, and, ultimately, peace to move forward in life.

So what is shaping your quest to find purpose in life? Is it the crisis you are stuck in today? Maybe it is strife, regret, or even a deep heartache you are trying to figure out for yourself or for a family member. In life, we all have obstacles that besiege us, but God tells us He will strengthen us to take us higher in our walk with Him. He will point the way. Jesus makes a promise to us in Matthew: "Take my yoke upon you and learn from me" (Matthew 11:29). In other words, "Become my disciple, because I am going to teach you how to carry it all." As you will find, God will always make a way out of your difficulty when you least expect it. You will discover who you are in Christ Jesus if you allow Him to walk with you down the path of forgiveness and inner healing. Are you ready?

At the end of each chapter, there is a "Time to Reflect" with questions to challenge those things that might be blocking a fulfilled life. Fear, doubt, sadness, despair, anxiety, worry, and rejection can all be replaced by the heavenly Father. His love will flush out your fears. His peace will displace your depression and anxiety. His gift of faith will replace your doubts. Hope will demolish despair. The joy of the Lord will sweep away any prolonged sadness. Every good gift is available to you through your Father. The most exquisite component to all of this is the Holy Spirit, Who will give you courage and strength to push through and will generously give you the wisdom in how to apply it. His voice will always lead you on the right path. This is what the prophet Joel proclaimed:

> In the last days, God says, I will pour out my Spirit on all people. Your sons and daughters will prophesy, your young men will see visions; your old men will dream dreams. Even on my servants, both men and women, I will pour out my Spirit in those days, and they will prophesy. I will show wonders in the heavens above and signs on the earth below, blood and fire and billows of smoke. The sun will be turned to darkness and the moon to blood before the coming of the great and glorious day of the Lord. And everyone who calls on the name of the Lord will be saved.

> *(Acts 2:17–21)*

Chapter 1

The Great and Terrible Last Day

*For the great day of their wrath has come, and
who can withstand it?*

—Revelation 6:17

One Friday morning in early December 2004, a Lutheran
pastor's name came up in conversation while my husband,
Paul, was attending a businessman's breakfast in New
Canaan, Connecticut. He was told the pastor lived in
Finland and was dying of lymphoma, which is a horrific
cancer. On the drive home, he felt he should contact the
pastor and ask if he wanted us to come and pray for
him. He found the ministry of the Finnish clergyman on
the Internet and also found one small button in the far
bottom right of the homepage of the website. It instructed
the reader to "Push here for English." Within a month,
an invitation was extended for us to travel to the small
European nation to pray and anoint this stricken man for

healing. He agreed to see us as soon as we could make travel arrangements, which our church board heartily approved of. It just so happened to be the dead of winter in the land of Finland.

As I peered out the window of our giant Boeing 747 as it landed at the Helsinki airport, it felt almost surreal. I was still pondering the ambitious thought that we would want to fly into one of the most northern countries on planet earth in the frigid winter. We certainly were not on any sight-seeing or vacation tour for this trip; instead, we were on a mission for God. A desperate Finnish pastor was in dire need of a touch from God, and we were praying to be used in any way we could.

You do not know my husband, but he takes life seriously as an ordained Lutheran pastor, and for forty-two years, he has kept an attentive ear to hear what God needs him to do, see the people he needs to minister to, and go to the places he needs to be when requested. As his partner in life and ministry, I stopped asking questions after so many years with him. One of my personal mottos (there are a few I adhere to) is to just "vacuum with my hat on" (meaning, to be ready for anything at the drop of a hat when the green light is signaled to go). It is an excellent motto, if you are adventurous and love life like he does. Thankfully, we are compatible in that sense.

Paul Teske also taught me through the years to trust that God is always right and knows what He is doing; when He asks us to be someplace or minister to someone in need, He loves our yes. I have admittedly learned a good lesson through many trials and, of course, many errors: that our God always wins, so it takes a lot of pressure off of any grumbling about the places I am traveling to, like observing this eerie landing in Finland through the small porthole of the plane. I could barely see the shape of the sun through the shrouded and hazy gray sky. Odd that it would be so dark in midmorning, I thought. I had read about these winters close to the North Pole but had never experienced one.

I decided on the spot that I was no Norsewoman and remembered to silently say a short prayer of thanksgiving that God thought it best that I hail from the great state of warmer and sunnier Texas (although I was displaced in Connecticut at the moment). I shivered a little and pulled the red blanket issued by the airline a little tighter around my shoulders.

Lost in thought for a few moments while the ground crew hustled the luggage out of the enormous aircraft, I let out a heavy sigh. Like we all try to do, I had been letting go of a few life issues that seemed to have plagued me for years with my family and with the spiritual community in parish ministry. It had been a hard-fought battle for my heart to let go and let God. Ugh, it means surrender. Those five simple words might just be the hardest to work through in life, but after seeing a sign from God in 2003, which you will read about in chapter 5, I had never been happier and more confident in working with Jesus on my personal healing journey. Not only had I fallen deeper in love with God, but I had also found a daily dialogue

3

and scripture study that took me from the mundane of existing to a crazy wild ride with the godhead.

Truthfully, I could not get enough during this initial season He and I were settling into. Maybe it was a reawakening or a reformation of the soul, which was taking me to higher mountaintops in the spiritual sense. It felt fabulous to be connected. Someone had recently prayed over me for a spine of steel. I had never heard of such a thing like praying steel into a spine, and at the moment, I thought it a little on the dramatic side of the prayer partner doing this.

On a lighter note, at least it sounded durable and indestructible. Currently, I needed that durability for ministry and life, and prayed that it was working. As eerie as the weather was outside, I sat back in my seat, feeling something had definitely changed inside of me. It is hard to explain in writing, but I felt lighter as we walked into the queue for foreign visitors. The sun never appeared again that day, but my heart was smiling. How odd to have a quick vision of a smiling heart, I thought. We were on a mission from God, and little did I know the mission would initially begin with my life being turned utterly upside down in a shattering time travel with God this very night.

A dear Finnish pastor who spoke very limited English met us at the airport. Our luggage barely fit into his tiny European Fiat, which also included me sitting in the back seat. Adjusting quickly to our new surroundings and the unbelievably frigid cold, I was captivated with the wintry sights as we made our way, winding slowly through snow and ice to get to the highway. We were driven to a very modest hotel in the commuter town of Jarvenpaa, just north of Helsinki.

As we passed the small Nordic towns along the way, I was curious about every detail of cultural life these tough people endured during the winter months. There were bundled shoppers actually pulling babies in sleds behind them, with long ropes attached to their waists. No visitor would find a proper English pram here in the marketplace. A maze of pathways cutting through mounds of snow also revealed cross-country skiers winding their way through the village streets on errands. I was fascinated to see a wall of skis lined up outside of the bakeries, cheese shops, and pubs, all standing like wooden toy soldiers awaiting their marching orders. How did each local resident know which pair might be theirs?

The young pastor mentioned how the Finns loved the ancient tradition of taking saunas and ice bath plunges. This nonsexual, invigorating health custom is where one takes a warm sauna and then plunges into a hole cut into a small ice area in a lake, then back to the sauna for hot drinks and more conversation. I was thankful there were no frozen lakes or ponds in the back of the small hotel. I might have been too shy to take the ice custom seriously.

We were invited to visit a Finnish high school that afternoon in the neighboring village and met the chaplain of the school, who was, of course, Lutheran. As you might already know, the state church of Finland is Lutheran;

how refreshing it was to see a chaplain in a school where the Catechism was taught, daily prayers were offered in classes, and Crosses hung along hallway walls. I also observed in detail that the students appeared to be extremely peaceful, happy, and healthy.

My first assumption could have attributed their disposition to the rugged outdoors and fresh air they breathed from the northern skies, but I learned that Finnish public schools were ranked as one of the top educational successes of the world, while her students held some of the highest overall test scores. Believe what you may, could it be that they succeeded mostly because God had not been taken out of their schools, classrooms, or hearts? The impact was refreshing to note, and I believe, wholeheartedly, the latter to be the actual truth. My prayer is that they will continue these core traditions and not allow the new political winds of the European Union to change their culture or moral laws.

Surprisingly, we were also entertained at the school by a traveling team of Christian college students from Switzerland, who gave a most remarkable interpretation of the Easter story, including the Cross. I once again had to reflect, compare, and offer my own opinion of our mediocre American educational system, where God had been declared dead in our schools since the 1970s. I am saddened to report that America has been ranked twenty-sixth in math and nineteenth in science in the industrialized world. Do I need to say more about this dismal report on America's schools? I should also mention that a good old-fashioned "Merry Christmas" cannot be shared in American schools, while here, a Cross from Switzerland was being talked about and the Resurrection dramatized to an enthusiastic Finnish student body.

Later that evening, after a treacherous walk to the village in our leather-soled American shoes, and an interesting and shocking menu selection of Finnish reindeer and other delicacies, we decided to take that sauna after returning to our little hotel. I decided that while in Rome, be a Roman. Why not? It was a Scandinavian delight, as promised in the tour books; however, I elected not to jump into the icy pool. I did not feel that adventurous but wondered how this tradition had been lost on the early Finnish immigrants to America. I believe we could have really benefitted from this healthy exercise in our culture.

The last surprise awaiting us that evening was the feathered down comforters on our beds. It had been an exhaustive travel day, and we were to leave early the next morning to drive to the northern Lapland area. I could hear the wind howling outside and the snow swirling around the windows as I dove further under the covers for protective warmth. "Ah!" The Europeans certainly had a cold winter's night down to a perfect sleeping science. I felt healthy, peaceful, and also happy as I fell off to dream. One last thing I do remember praying was, "Thank You, too, Father God, for a new smile upon my heart." Tomorrow would be here too soon.

During the night, I awakened out of an incredibly deep

sleep to what sounded like millions of people screaming near the small hotel. The horrific sound jolted me wide awake. My first thought was that people were marching around outside of the hotel to find and kill the Teskes. I panicked, thinking, *Why did they want to bother with us?* We were just here to pray for a Lutheran pastor. I remember thinking that I did not want to die a horrible death on foreign soil.

After my mind cleared of the initial shock, and feeling fairly certain that we were not under siege, I heard an audible male voice whisper into my ear. I knew that voice. I was becoming more familiar with the inflections and tones in our daily conversations we were engaged in. It was the Father's voice, and He was speaking to me in those early morning hours right here in Finland.

He instructed me to keep my eyes closed and announced that He was showing me the Great and Terrible Last Day. "What?" My body was immobilized like a bag of cement. That fast. Frozen. I could not move one muscle, not even my mouth. What was God going to show me, and why in the world did He want to show me this? (After the vision was finished, I recalled many references to the Last Day and the Second Coming in scripture. I would have to look all of these up at a later time.)

Of course, I had no time to think through what I could recall, as this epic vision commenced as quickly as I had heard the voice. Let me first begin by giving the definition of the words *great* and *terrible* from *Webster's Dictionary*. *Great* is an adjective that denotes the element of something that is most important, most worthy of consideration, an event or subject of importance or impressively large. *Terrible* is defined as "dreadful, awful, appalling, horrific, horrifying, horrible, horrendous, atrocious, abominable, deplorable, egregious, abhorrent, frightful, shocking, hideous, ghastly, grim, dire, unspeakable, gruesome, monstrous, sickening, heinous, vile, serious, grave, acute." I was witness to all of the above descriptive meanings in an epic vision, which incorporated immense sound, sight, and deep emotion, as you will read. Still to this day, I am unquestionably curious and profoundly humbled that I was given this incredible privilege to see this, but why me? And what was I supposed to do with it?

With eyes closed as instructed, I was immediately brought into a breathtaking panoramic view of planet earth, which opened up onto an expansive azure blue sky blanketing the earth as far as I could see to the horizon. The heavens opened, and as I looked to the east and then to the west, I was acutely aware that I was standing here alone. There were no markers to tell me the exact location. The brilliant azure color of the sky above stunned my visual senses, as it was a combination of turquoise, lapis blue, sapphire, and a blue that one might find in a virgin ocean unscathed with trash or muck. It was a collective color of all these blues, but not of this world.

My attention was abruptly refocused by the sounds of massive roars of waves somewhere in the distance, although I did not see an ocean. The great sounds were walls of deep, oceanic waters parting somewhere in the atmosphere overhead. I strained to see if I could get a glimpse of anything that might resemble a white cloud or the deafening body of colossal waters that I heard. I saw nothing except planet earth swathed in blue.

As sudden as the cloudless roar subsided, a blanket of soundless air covered the earth, and just as the blanket hit, there was an imposing and dramatic note of a trumpet, which blasted an announcement in the sky. The blast made me jump a little (maybe I jumped a lot). Where did that sound come from? It bathed the entire earth as one, lone sound of air pushed up from the lungs of an unearthly giant, heralding all humanity to come to attention. The note came from somewhere out in the universe, although I could not see the trumpet or the person playing it. Almost like a dramatic cosmic stage effect, I sensed an invisible velvet drape from heaven sweep back, announcing the magnificent appearance of the reigning main character.

And there He was. Jesus the Christ, the One, appeared in the expansive sky. His entrance was so dramatic and so overpowering, I wanted to fall on my face with the holiness and overwhelming purity of the light that shrouded Him. I was singularly transfixed on His person and image. Have you ever wondered how people from across the world will know when Jesus comes on the Day of the Lord, as scripture promises? Let me assure you, all of humanity will know the exact moment He appears. As I write out this awesome vision in the sky, I am reminded of the great Hallelujah chorus from the *Messiah* that we sing at Christmas, with its soaring crescendos preceding the great ending of the sacred piece. I wanted to shout this Hallelujah to the skies above while standing and waiting for whatever was going to take place next. In Matthew 24, Jesus tells us the signs of the end of the age:

> *Then will appear the sign of the Son of Man in heaven. And then all the peoples of the earth will mourn when they see the Son of Man coming on the clouds of heaven, with power and great glory. And he will send his angels with a loud trumpet call, and they will gather his elect from the four winds, from one end of the heavens to the other.*
>
> *(Matthew 24:30–31)*

The godhead (God the Father, God the Son, and God the Holy Spirit) was altogether so holy and too extravagant for me to take it in all at once. How can I describe such majesty as He took His stand in the sky as the resplendent King of Kings? Did I suck my breath in and hold it? I felt as if I could not breathe, as I stood mesmerized in this space and time. Jesus's feet were literally touching the earth's entire vortex, and His head was reaching far above the atmosphere. It was as if His entire being engulfed the towering space.

Forgive me, but my description seems so feeble in human terms, even as I write. He is indescribable but radiant, with handsome features, regal with unmatched stature and posture. His eyes projected earth's powerful fullness, with atomic energy yet to be unleashed, but His captivating eyes were of pure love. How could these two elements collide with such force? I remember thinking I had never seen such pure love. I desperately wanted to touch the love with a gentle hand. I was totally bathed in this pureness like a cocoon, but then I saw something so formidable that it caused me to look away for just one moment. I still get choked up and must pause when I reread this portion and remember His eyes. They were filled with the most unfathomable sorrow. I wanted to weep and weep for Him, but I could not.

The deepest and most intense pain I had ever felt hit my chest, knocking the breath out of me. I could hardly bear the weight of His sorrow. I felt as if I had taken a Herculean punch in the stomach, and again, I caught myself wanting to collapse and fall face down to the ground to bow to this Holiness.

Implausible as it might sound, I realized Jesus was allowing me a small glimpse of His own grieving emotions behind the power surge in His eyes. I believe it was the heavy weight of the final destiny of the unbelieving humans before Him, resting so heavily on His shoulders, which was crushing my ribs. My heart was breaking for Him and the world, while my mind was racing. It was like listening to twenty radio programs simultaneously. I immediately thought of all those in front of me who were lost in unbelief and rebellion, never to recover after this final judgment. Can final destiny even be captured as a riveting look of grief, or was I just imagining this demise? Whatever it was, why would Jesus allow me to feel this great pity and unspeakable sorrow upon those who had rejected Him, once and for all? What was He trying to show me? This question still haunts me today, as it did from the unveiling of the vision. I was emotionally ruined at this point, but more came. He would not allow me to turn aside and run, but I wanted to.

His Clothing

The Great Master was adorned in a rich and royal robe that was blindingly white. Straight from the tailor's shop, it seemed. I certainly don't want to sound flippant as I describe this, but I have often wondered why His robes were never wrinkled in my visions or dreams. Such a silly manufacturer's thought, I know, but very true. Of course, they would have to be the best clothes in the business. After all, He was God. A beautiful, pure gold linen sash crossed the chest. There was precious metal woven in thousands of exquisite strands through the linen fabric, and I could see His powerful feet in leather sandals peeking out from under the hem of the majestic covering. Although I could not see His arms, I could imagine how powerful they were underneath the bell sleeves as He lifted both hands up into the sky like a blessing, or was this some kind of signal He was giving to His angels?

The Angels

Flanking Jesus on the right and left side were Michael and Gabriel, the archangels of God. They were mighty creatures in their own right, resplendent and awesome in beauty, but no match for the Holy One that stood between these giants. Behind Jesus and the archangels, stacked up in thousands of rows into the outer limits of the heavens, stood the legion forces, called the warring angels. Multimillions is a humble estimate, which sounds so bizarre to try and count out, but you need the epic numbers to understand the enormity of these forces I was seeing for the first time in my life. They seemed to be clones of one another. I knew immediately who they were and felt that we, as the people of God, should never have been fearful of one thing while living on earth. Why had we not been stronger and more courageous in fighting evil? They had been our protectors, working for and with God to surround us when in dire need and in trouble and, of course, in all of life.

Again, human language fails, as I try to fully describe these incredible warriors to you. They were an odd mixture of half-male and heavenly combination with facial features of eyes, nose, mouth, and ears. They were gold and shiny in color, colossal in height, but extremely slender. I am not a good judge of height, but maybe they stood fifteen or twenty feet high. There was a vibrant essence about their bodies, shimmering as if extraordinary energy rushed in and out of their veins and into their expansive golden wings. I could hear the sound of this shimmering life and the sound of their wings, which made a swishing sound: the only thing that barely moved in the stillness of the incredible scene. As awesome as the bodies of these warring angels were, it was the fierceness in their eyes that I could not look away from. Their eyes captivated me with such intense focus that I wanted to stand and study them.

There was only one thing in their line of sight, and that was their General. I knew Jesus Christ was their leader, the Commander-in-Chief, the Conqueror, and with one word uttered from His mouth to His army, I knew they could and would destroy for Him. They were on a mission. I sensed they were acutely aware of humanity standing before them like small grasshoppers. I sure felt like one, under their visual line. I no longer was alone, but now looking around, I was aware of standing with billions of human beings in the earthly space. I wanted to make sure my children, my grandchildren, and my husband were nearby. I could not see them, but I knew they were there. Here we were (God's people), looking up at the Creator God and His Creation (the angels). From the wealthiest to the poorest, kings and queens standing next to the servant, adult to child, every nation, every color of humanity under heaven, billions upon billions of women, men, and children, standing breathlessly before Jesus. It was a staggering thought, and I was once again aware of the immense space of the sky and the color of blue. Was it always this vast to the human eye? Was it always this blue? It was not at all important at this point, but later, as I recalled the incalculable details, I thought it might have been cool to know exactly where I had been standing on earth as this was all unveiled. It was something I would have marked, thought about, and remembered to look for on every map or globe.

Time

Everything on planet earth then abruptly stopped. No birds sang. No crickets chirped. Where were they? The thickened silence was deafening to my ears, which felt like they were bursting from surround sound. It felt as if the life was being sucked out of the desolation, much like I experienced on the tragic day in New York City, which will forever be called 9/11 in history.

I distinctly remembered the numbing silence of the city once the Twin Towers had fallen; air traffic had been halted, and the thousands of citizens who had poured over the streets and bridges made it to safety. We were all shocked, trying to comprehend the insanity of terrorists and realizing how the world would never be the same again. Time had seemed to stop in slow motion as the entire world watched the news in horror. Yes, the world had changed that day, and now the world was changing again, in front of my eyes. Maybe the sound of silence was what caused me to hear the breath of humankind trying not to breathe. Maybe we were trying to hold our breath so as not to scream. It was an oxymoron.

Whatever the case, an earth-shattering domino effect suddenly crossed the expansive landscape of the noiseless planet we were all standing on. The ground shook with a reverberating thunderous swell, as the knee of every inhabitant hit the ground with sheer force to bow before King Jesus. I cannot be sure, but I imagine this colossal sound of every knee hitting the ground could be felt around the globe and unsettled everyone to the core, as it did me. The sound of the domino effect was indeed shattering.

The Name

It must have been the first time in the history of creation that humankind spoke as with one voice. In one historical, epic moment, we humbly bowed before the Savior of the universe and call out for mercy. Of course, it should have been this way from the beginning of time. Why did we have the incredible desire for human power century upon century? Why the insatiable desire to proudly sin against God? The greed, the wars, the idolatry, the spilling of innocent blood, the narcissistic holocaust of humanity all made me nauseous to consider while on bended knee before Him. We had indeed brought this Day of Judgment upon ourselves.

All we needed to do was repent and call upon the name of the Lord. He has told us so often throughout many scriptures: "And everyone who calls on the name of the Lord will be saved." Acts 2:21. I believe the extraordinary sadness I had seen multiplied by the billions in His eyes was the stark truth that humankind had let Him down. I myself wanted to crumble at the moment in a deep river of sadness. However, who could fathom His ways or think like Him? He was our Father and in love with us. At the very moment of wanting to die before God, I felt love pour over me like waves of silk. He must have known I needed the reassurance of love to sustain what was happening around me in such swift motion.

The atmosphere exuded holy reverence and awe while we were on bended knee. In one elongated, harmonic voice, the name "Jesus, Jesus, Jesus" was pronounced three bold times from our lips in unison. Between each proclamation of the name, "Jesus," there was a significant pause. Each time the breath of all humanity declared His Name in one unified voice, it created a shock wave of cosmic proportion, like an atomic bomb blast. Its circuitous ripple effect of rings hit Jesus and the angelic hosts wave after wave when we said, "Jesus." Their bodies swayed slightly back in rhythmic unison under the weight of our human voice. Even their wings moved ever so slightly from the blast.

The Death Knell

What happened next was the terrible I defined above. Read the definition over if you must. Immediately, the throngs of people who had mocked His name, spit in His face, and hated Him with their evil and black hearts became restless. Those who had disavowed their relationship with Him and aligned themselves with Satan, those who were narcissistic and worshipped vile imaginations with their lifestyles and cultural wars, were now totally obsolete. The very "rights of man" they had ferociously fought for through the ages were meaningless, useless, and hopeless, and now it all became nonexistent at this point. I remembered the depressing words of King Solomon in Ecclesiastes: "meaningless, meaningless, utterly all is meaningless." I could sense their quickening demise. The "gnashing of teeth" that the Bible speaks of on that Last Day had begun. They knew they were doomed to hell and eternal destruction. These liars, cheats, idol worshipers, and disobedient, lustful, and carnal creatures were still completely unrepentant to the core and a disgusting abomination to God now. I could not believe their arrogance and stubbornness, as eternal hell stared them in the face. It was so shocking that the human will could think it was strong enough to take on God.

The unfathomable sorrow I had witnessed earlier in His eyes for humanity was now gone. Something that struck me at the time haunts me to this day, as I recall the scene. I could hear their minds trying to grasp the enormity of the eternal destruction and punishment of hell they were doomed for. Was this the hideous and horrific sound that had first awakened me before the vision began? A deep wail from the weakening souls, which I will call the death knell, caused me to tremble on the spot. The brains of the doomed were actually screaming and exploding inside their heads but staying intact, as they called out the name of the Holy Jesus one last time.

I will use a defendant's day in court with the judge as an example of what was transpiring in the natural. As you know, the gavel is hammered on the formidable bench of the judge, and the final verdict from the head juror pronounces, "Guilty." Many in the courtroom might gasp or celebrate, with an understated joy. The eternal reality faced by the masses was nothing like the human drama in court, but it had the same appalling effect released upon humanity's hopelessness. I felt an absolutely overwhelming helplessness at this point for the millions about to be destroyed. I should have worked harder to bring the Gospel to more people. I felt, too, that I fit into every category their restlessness portrayed. Had I failed one person? Oh God, please tell me I did not let one person down who might have believed. I am certain that I did. I felt wretched while wrapped in the scene before me. I wanted to weep and scream myself that I had blown it for a searching soul's questions that I might have answered. I prayed that someone else had taken up my uncaring slack. No one at this moment in history would have wished even a foe to endure what was happening. I felt horrified for what was about to take place for them. But as humbling as the terrible was, it was also the great day of the Lord for the people who believed. However, I did not see one believer rejoice in any outwardly manner. The moment was too holy, too forgiving, and too introspective of one's own intense reality to make a move of joy. By the very grace of God, I could only sense the overwhelming thankfulness and shout of praise and thanksgiving in the hearts of the believers, which also included myself.

The Vision Lifted

I lay in the simple Finnish twin bed, not able to move. My breath was coming in gulps. My lungs were bursting to breathe air. Had I been holding my breath through the entire epic experience? "Dear God," was all I could mouth while lying there. It took a few minutes to return to the reality of the small hotel room. Thank You, God; I was alive. I was shaking from head to toe under those feather blankets and not because of the frigid northern winds. In the moment, I was moved by sheer gratitude, humility, joy, and relief. Relief, in the fact that I knew Jesus, certainly everyone knew Him when they saw Him taking up the entire earth's blue sky. The relief that I was known by the Almighty God Himself overwhelmed me. Jesus knew me. I was saved from the bloodbath about to take place.

That was and is the difference, you see. The difference is that He knows you and knows me on the Last Day. I immediately remembered He had known us from the beginning of time and had created each one of us in our mother's womb in His holy image. I felt an unabashed thankfulness wash over me. Jesus knew me as His very own daughter, and I was indebted. The scriptures tell us we are not our own. I really don't know if there's another word that can capture the incomprehensible essence of gratitude as I lay in that bed near the North Pole. You can fill in the blanks with your own deep reflection. Hallelujah! I think I said, "Thank You, Jesus," over two hundred times in the early hours of that new day. "Thank You that I have the Holy Spirit, which resides in me because of all that You are."

I also lay there, humbly thanking all the unnamed persons who had prayed me into the unseen Kingdom. I would never know the ancestors, friends, prayer warriors, or unknown strangers who knew God well before I was born, and yet, somehow, I knew they had prayed for me and future generations to come to Christ. I have done this myself by praying for my grandchildren and the legacy that will follow in our family. I thanked God that He knew me before the foundations of the earth were laid and that He loved me enough to send the Messiah to save me and every saint from the gates of hell, which I had just about witnessed. He knew my name, "Rivers," and that, my dear friend, is my ultimate prayer for you. "Thank You, Father," I prayed, "that my name is written in the Lamb's Book of Life and that I belong to You."

I slowly opened my eyes and squinted to see the tiny European timepiece hanging to my left. It took several seconds in the darkened, winterized room for my eyes to adjust, but when they did, the little clock on the wall read 3 a.m. In slow motion, I also turned my head on the pillow slightly higher to see if Paul had heard what I just witnessed. He was lightly snoring. I pulled the covers tighter around me to ask God over and over why He had shown the Great and Terrible to me. Who in the world was I? I was just an ordinary woman who had made a trip with my husband to pray for a dying soul. I was a speck on planet earth, like those grasshoppers. Why me? The $64,000 question still remains with me, to this very day.

I had many questions that early morning and over the years since the Great and Terrible was revealed. I've thought of the vision often and told a handful of faithful friends what was revealed in those early hours in 2004. They have all encouraged me to write it down for you. The vision is as vivid today as it was that cold, wintry morning in Finland. I am still astonished and captivated by every scene as I read and reread this chapter. God had stopped the vision before I saw the ending of humankind. Why? What might have happened? Were the unbelievers thrown into the fiery waters of hell, to be destroyed on that very day? Were they burned and annihilated from sight, like Sodom and Gomorrah? Or did the Son of Man speak to the throngs and then give the warring angels standing behind Him the command to destroy?

It obviously was not for me to see or to know. The part and parcel that I did witness was a justifiable life-changing event and enough to carry me through to the end of my time here on earth. I was just relieved to still have time on earth to do something for God. I pray that you will do just one small thing for humankind in kindness and love, to change something that could bring Christ to a dying person, to a village, to a town, to a nation, to a lost world. Better yet, will you do something to change yourself?

Tomorrow may be too late for someone who might be waiting for a word or a touch or even love. Do not let the sun go down if you need to tell someone just three more things to bring hope and restoration to them.

I was rather shocked as we went to pray for the Lutheran pastor with cancer that morning. What a trip, and it had been less than twenty-four hours since landing near the North Pole. I felt as if all energy had been drained out of me during the drive. Sitting in the back seat of the little Fiat, I contemplated long and hard about telling the pastor we were visiting everything concerning this vision. I remember trying, but it might have been lost in translation somehow.

We were ushered into a small office of the local sports arena, where he held church services for thousands on Sundays. Obviously, something was going on with this great ministry in the Lapland. We were thanked for coming all this way to pray and were told the meeting would be fairly short due to the exhaustion of the patient. As we sat down with the pastor, his assistant, and our Finnish driver and translator, Paul stated in a matter-of-fact voice that God had given him a word and scripture regarding the cancer in his body on the flight over, which would confirm our meeting. Paul then announced to the pastor and the small circle of Finns that "he has no cancer in his body" and that the scripture he had been given for the visit was Romans 4:17.

Wow. I was totally flabbergasted that he could make such a daring and bold proclamation to this poor man, who looked as if he might die on the spot. I sat motionless, and horror probably crossed my face for a split-second, as I tried not to fall out of my chair. I hoped it had not been seen, as I did not want anything to disrupt the great faith of healing that my husband had for this stage 4 cancer patient. The scripture that Paul had received regarding the meeting was the very passage they too had received just two days earlier, confirming our visit. Now, it was the Finns who might have wanted to fall out of their chairs.

You can imagine the atmosphere dripped with the Glory of God after this miracle. I believe we were all awestruck with the enormity of the situation and God's unbelievable timing for this trip. Paul suggested we take Communion for covenant worship in community and for an even deeper healing of His holy sacrament for our bodies and souls. We have always totally believed in the healing power of Communion, which is one of the great tenets of our Christian faith. The team had to scrounge around for the elements of unleavened bread and wine, as the Lutheran bishops in Finland had forbidden the pastor in exile from participating in Holy Communion with the congregants of his sports arena church. The team found a few crackers and juice somewhere in the hall that we could consecrate and take. It turned out to be a glorious few hours as the color crept back into the cancer-free skin of the sick man in front of us. Maybe it was the infusion of the healing power of Communion and the awesome presence of God that we felt covering our time together.

We left the cold and striking countryside of Finland

a few days later and will always remember its unique beauty and people. We attended the church of the Finnish pastor who had traveled with us and spoke that evening in the little town of Jarvenpaa. I shall always thank God that He gave us this extra opportunity, as we were blessed to worship with real gypsies (in full traditional costume, wielding their merry tambourines) and a group who outwardly loved the Lord. We never know the surprises God might have waiting when we say yes to His mission trips.

It was several weeks later that we received an email from the very embarrassed Lutheran pastor in exile." He indeed had been given a clean bill of health the Friday before our visit and had been in such shock when Paul pronounced him cancer free. Only his wife, his assistant, and the physicians knew that the tests were showing negative results. There was absolutely no cancer in his body. He apologized profusely that he had not said so in our meeting.

Time to Reflect

1. When you think about the return of Christ as I encountered in this vision, what emotions are stirred up?
2. When Jesus returns, are you prepared to meet Him?

Scripture Study

1. Read Ephesians 2:8–9; focus on the words *faith, grace, works,* and *gift.* What do they mean to you in the context of this passage?
2. Read Romans 8:37–39. Are you fully convinced that nothing will ever separate you from the love of God in Christ Jesus?

Chapter 2

Matters of the Heart

*Music gives a soul to the universe, wings to
the mind, flight to the imagination, and life to
everything.*

—*Plato*

I want to start where the narrative actually begins, so you
will understand how I reached the point of what some
would call the dark night of the soul. Not all is gloomy,
but I faced several challenges that impacted my life, and
God ultimately invaded it to save my lost soul. My hope
is that if you are going through a devastating trial or a
hardship, you will be drawn to the healing power of God
and the Spirit to get you through. It took years for me to
acknowledge that I could trust God and people in general,
because I simply did not want to be disappointed to find
out that I didn't matter to anyone as an individual. I was
isolated, in pain, and had forgotten that friends might be

there to support and raise me up in prayer. Both my self-image and self-worth needed deeper healing. I came to understand that there are two critical and basic questions that all of civilization struggles with: Am I loved, and why am I on earth?

I want to be upfront that this is not a biography but a way in which I could weave integrated life experiences into a story of personal healing and empowerment through the Spirit. I had to come to a crossroad in life and decide, did the heavenly Father love me or want me, and did I have a specific purpose in Kingdom work? This book presents eight dramatic visions (one of which you have just read), compelling dreams, and a significant sign God used to invade my life on my journey. They are as important for you today as they were for me. At the time, I had no idea that God still speaks to His people as He did in the Old and New Testament. Consequently, I have read many commentaries on the subject of visions and dream language, concluding that we serve an awesome God of signs, wonders, and miracles, and as His people, we are right in the middle of the conversation with Him.

Early Life

I cannot remember when I first fell in love with music, or whether it fell in love with me. It just seemed to be trapped inside of my body somewhere. At three, I vividly remember a favorite old hymn of most young churchgoers.

I am sure you have heard it sung hundreds of times from a variety of musical artists. The lyrics simply say:

"Jesus loves me this I know, for the Bible tells me so. Little ones to Him belong, they are weak, but He is strong. Yes, Jesus loves me. Yes, Jesus loves me. Yes, Jesus loves me. The Bible tells me so."

I loved to sing this little piece and belted it out in my Sunday best voice each week on the front pew of the "cradle row," as they called the children's section at the church we attended. Music became a part of my life and a way I could escape the maddening loneliness and sadness I struggled with. This little ditty was surely the beginning of that love affair.

By about seven years old, my young mind was not so sure about the love or belonging part of the children's song. There were two underlying circumstances that shaped my early life. First, the harsh reality of waking up in the mornings without an intact family in our home devastated me. I needed to be surrounded by love and security, not abandonment and rejection. When I was five, my biological father divorced my mother and left her with three small children. The indelible mark of shame and confusion upon each of our young hearts left us adrift. It was the late 1950s, a time in American history that was extremely edgy for single mothers and hardest for me to cope with in the elementary school under the duress of knowing that we might be considered odd or unusual in the neighborhood.

My mother struggled in those early years, as she

had to work outside of the home and had to hire several housekeepers, women who did their best to oversee our daily care. As the oldest, I became very good at being the second mother: self-reliant, probably too responsible, and unconsciously assigned the role of hero child and fixer in our enmeshed family system. I found many of these more adult responsibilities caused extreme nervousness at a young age, which I learned to hide quite well.

Marriage and divorce were handled differently in the 1950s than today. One of the most damaging issues that I would deal with most of my life was a severe fear of abandonment (physical and emotional) and the inability to fully trust a man who made promises that could not be kept. I only saw my biological father a few times until I was twelve and after that, maybe three in my entire lifetime. My mother gave him the nickname Santa Claus, which stuck until his death. After his third wife, I decided that we were just not that important to him, after all.

During the 1950s, our favorite shows happened to be *Father Knows Best* and *My Three Sons*. I would sit mesmerized in front of our small black-and-white television and long for a dinner table or a lap to sit on, which included a dad in our lives. These two early sitcoms must have had a profound impact on many people growing up in those more idyllic years, as they are frequently referenced in stories we hear in our counseling offices today. Through extensive research on the family, inner healing, and prayer ministry, Paul and I have found that paternal absenteeism and the effect of the father's love on the family unit is critical to the emotional health and physical well-being of each child. If not dealt with earlier than later, it can have long-lasting and devastating effects on the heart. I know in the earlier years of youth, I struggled with not having a father or the validation of love and affirmation.

Thank God my mother fell in love with my "forever" father when I was eight. He must have been so brave in his mid-twenties to take on the responsibility as a father figure to care for three small children and a new wife. He worked hard as a successful young engineer and grew to corporate leadership in a few short years. But through all those years as a parent, there was just one thing he could never bring himself to do: He could not say, "I love you," or "I am so proud of you and what you have accomplished." As many of his generation, which I will give him a pass on, he provided love in many other areas of our life. He provided care, was generous for anything we asked for, attended our sports games, and paid for us all to go to college; he left the parenting to my mother and was a man of very few words. But in his quiet dialogue, three words escaped him. Just three words or eight simple letters could have covered a multitude of sins and protectively changed the emotional canvas of our lives, our hearts, and our family. It would not be until his deathbed, the last two weeks of his life, that he told us he loved us. How sad to think we all had to wait over fifty-seven years to hear those beautiful words. I often reflect on why it's so hard for people to verbally express love. Love could change the world, you know. Families, communities, and nations could all use a massive dose of the verbal word-in-action.

By the time I turned eleven, there were five kids to feed, clothe, get to school, and schedule appointments for. I was the oldest sibling and often took the brunt of the disciplinary action on many occasions and simply believed the far-flung accusation at times: "You are just like your father." I actually had no idea what my birth father was like, but it slowly dawned on me through those years, and in a counselor's office much later in life, the statement was a cruel and abusive comparison I had believed and felt ashamed for. Sadly, that ugly judgmental association and the multilayered effects of divorce in the mid-1950s left indelible marks upon my young trusting heart; I grew up in a household that was silently sad and unable to communicate together to resolve issues. We were all aching from needing more emotional health than we had. After years in research and extensive training in family systems and dynamics, the health care community has come to learn that children are easily used as pawns in tumultuous, angry adult relationships. If these imprinted messages are not dealt with and healed, one can be set up for a lifetime of problems and issues. My recipe for success became excessive striving while skillfully throwing myself into the music that I loved.

The second circumstance that affected me unwittingly was the abusive spiritual background I was raised in. It would take years to understand the emotional toll and the spiritual emptiness, loneliness, and mistrust I experienced because of this. After reflecting on those years during some intense counseling, I discovered the greatest wall of fear was that of God and men in authority. I do not like to speak ill of churches, but the hellfire from the old pulpit preacher we had to listen to was often interspersed with control, manipulation, and self-proclaimed authoritative discourse. My grandmother, my mother, my two great-aunts, and their families attended this church, where we must have all felt rejected by God, who was the Judge of the universe on any occasion.

I recall my sweet grandfather (who would not have stepped on an ant) sitting in the back pew, usually designated for the backsliders (I hated that terminology and its intended invisible shaming). I often wondered how he must have felt all those years from the blasting sermons because he never ventured from his "stall," as he called it. He was the kindest, most caring, and gentlest person who ever walked planet earth. Maybe he tuned out the pulpit proclamations to think of other things.

My father also chose not to attend services with us, but I could not blame him. I certainly did not want to be there myself. Salvation was never talked about in terms of grace, mercy, or the love of Jesus. The old pastor could not even bring himself to like the popular Billy Graham. He would rant about him in fiery sermons sometimes weeks on end. Who could not like Billy? He was out saving the world in venues called crusades. As I became older and a little more insightful, I believe it might have been some kind of deep-seated jealousy he held secretly against the charismatic evangelist. Of course, I did walk the aisle for Jesus and repentance out of guilt at least once a quarter and was finally asked to leave the church choir at thirteen because my skirt measured two inches above the kneecaps. I am sure it would be considered religious abuse today to kneel on a floor with a measuring stick, although there was no such name for it then. I was devastated not to sing, but out of pure spite, I did not lower my hems. I fought my mother and not so silently rejoiced when she finally left this peculiar environment. I never looked back and left for college three years later. It felt like freedom to actually think on my own and verbalize opinions without serious ramifications. Honestly, we had almost been suffocated as a family by that church's controlled insanity. Leaving it was the best thing that could have happened to us.

In the somewhat tumultuous teenage years that most youth manage to live through, I sought my friendships in music, beauty pageants, and every office I could run for in school. "Vote Clean Air & Rivers" was my branded logo for each campaign. In today's political and global arena, I imagine my slogan of climate awareness could continue to stand as a winner. I was runner-up to Miss Texas in 1976 and loved the people of Texas I met along the way. There is just no one like a Texan, and it was one of the best years of my life. After the pageant, I began a rigorous schedule preparing for my senior recital at Baylor University and was accepted to the Music Conservatory in Graz, Austria, for vocal training in opera. If a young American singer had any aspirations on the world stage,

Europe was the first training ground to build political and career savvy in the industry. I was prepared and eager to have this opportunity to spread my wings in a new and adventurous life and pretty sure my DNA included a strong travel and adventure gene somewhere in the family legacy.

But God, whom I did not think much about except on Sundays, must have had other plans, because a very tanned, handsome young clergyman came to town on his way from Central America to his last year in seminary. He sat with a mutual friend at the restaurant where I worked. This was not a typical-looking preacher, for whatever I thought that might mean, and neither was the restaurant where I worked a typical eating establishment. We sang show tunes and short operettas while serving steaks to patrons and, of course, the proverbial "Happy Birthday" song, which I belted out with flair and fluff, hitting the high C for extra gratuities, filling the coffers for my new European adventure coming up. The young clergyman spilled his milk and left me a ten-dollar tip that day. I thought it was an overly generous fortune for one to leave for a lunch. Who could have even dreamt that I would entertain going out with this "preacher man," as our mutual friend called him?

Well, the preacher was actually in town for four extra days, waiting on his fancy red sports car he had ordered for his senior year. Obviously, his occupation was never on my radar to give any inordinate amount of thought to, until he asked me out. Do you know of any young girl who has ever been asked out on a date by a man of the cloth? Maybe you do, but not many. Of course, I did not know of any, nor did my three roommates, who insisted on taking me to the ER for my head to be examined when I said yes to his proposal.

My poor grandmother was the other casualty of this dating scenario. She had what one would call a Texas fit because he was Lutheran, and somewhere in her narrow circle of biblical philosophy, Lutherans were equated to Catholics. It was a little hypocritical and unforgiving on her part, as certain members of our family (on my father's side) were also of the Catholic persuasion. "Wasn't that religion like the pope?" she inquired. She made it very clear to him after the two had met that in no way was he to interrupt what the family (the women) had been grooming me for, which was the operatic stage. This was an unspoken law that no one should ever cross the line with.

Two things stand out as I recall her elaborate consternation. First, too many institutions of faith just never collaborate in unity for any reason other than the fact that tradition stands as belief, which is to say, a terrible reason because the church could actually defeat the enemy on every social issue of the days in which we live. Second, the matriarchal control she hammered out for the family was totally dysfunctional. End of story.

Need I tell you that I never made it to Graz, Austria, but became Mrs. Paul Teske the next year, much to the chagrin of many? I am honestly sure my family and friends laid bets on how long I would last in the business as a poverty-stricken parish pastor's wife. Most thought I had lost my way and my mind. In the early days of parish ministry and my nerves, I might have genuinely agreed I had chosen the road less traveled. It is definitely unique fieldwork and not for the faint of heart, but I had Paul, and the initial adventure with him was just getting started. I would need him to guide me with his strength and courage.

With two hundred dollars to our name, we set out on our new life as a couple. God certainly had a sense of humor in picking me out of the several others who wanted to be his wife. I often chuckle, remembering those days and how I managed to be seen as a leader of a flock of church people. Either I was a pretty good actress (which I was) or had a legacy of early American settlers (which I did), because our first assignment was to a small, rural farming community in Ohio. As I struggled to find my place in the community, there was a tremendous amount of simple love and leeway from older members of the congregation, who helped me circumvent the bumps. Thank goodness very few management skills were needed at the time on my part, but intuition and sheer German and English gut must have helped keep me precariously balanced. As a college graduate from a large city, I could, in fact, spell the title, Clergy Wife, but I would have to learn how to enjoy canning tomatoes, putting up pickles, and making baklava my first year on the job if I was going to get to know the church ladies. Missionary work was not an easy proposition if one did not have a perspective on Jesus. It was the perspective on Jesus that I was trying to figure out.

Candidly, I would say the first year of our marriage was rocky and stormy; Paul and I were naïve and trying to figure out this new lifestyle and one another. I actually ran away twice (only to the next town) to cry on a friend's shoulder (another pastor's wife). To be honest, my friend and I could not have handled the pressure of parish ministry without one another to lean on. In life, you don't have to handle an issue alone if you can find one trusted friend to walk shoulder to shoulder with. It is a rare treasure if you can find that. She was a treasure trove of acceptance as we shared the interesting sphere of influence we both had.

In the fall of 1977, I auditioned for the Cleveland Symphony with the famous maestro, Lorin Maazel. After choosing a favorite Puccini aria at nine months and two weeks pregnant, I shockingly sang and hit the high B-flat with no trouble at all and was driven straight to the hospital that evening to deliver a baby girl. On stage, the conductor told me he wanted to personally drive me the one hundred miles, as he had never heard such a glorious sound from such a pregnant female. Thankfully, the baby had dropped preparing for birth, so I could reach those soaring notes at the end of the dramatic audition.

As much as I loved the stage and adored performing opera, I hoped my new daughter was going to love music, as she certainly had listened to the sounds of organs, orchestras, and her mother's voice for nine months. She and I were going to be buddies in the opera companies I sang with; even behind the curtains, stagehands snuggled with her. Sigh. Opera: I loved the drama of it all. If you are not familiar with operatic librettos, they are dramatic ballads set to orchestral compositions composed by the masters of the seventeenth- and eighteenth-century music world and interlaced with gloriously overrated stories of heroines and heroes. Most are twisted with deception, gossip, gun duels, and opulent lifestyles, which most often offer a good death scene of some sort in the final minutes. A little depressing, I admit, but I was caught up in the magical aspect of stage performance and wondered how I was going to balance career with a family.

In 1979, while singing in Cleveland and finding my political prowess with several opera companies in the area, the Office of Active Duty Military Chaplaincy in Washington DC sent orders for Paul to report for active duty. We both had a patriotic love for our country from childhood and thought that change, coupled with military service and protocol, would be something we'd thoroughly enjoy in life. He said yes to the call, and I said yes to the anticipated adventure of going to an American port city with historical roots. With mixed emotions, we left our first parish ministry in rural Ohio. We also left the comfort of dear families who had given us the gift of simple love and acceptance as a young, married couple in a farming and steel mill environment. We drove to our new duty station at the Naval Hospital in Philadelphia, two years older and a little wiser, I hoped. We were excited to forge a new chapter in our lives, and I hoped to adapt quickly to life as a Navy chaplain and officer's wife at the hospital. Have I mentioned that I was on cruise control with God at the time?

Surely, this new move was going to be just what I needed to find happiness and an inner peace. While we waited for our small shipment of furniture to arrive, we were treated to the exciting annual Army-Navy football game across the street from the hospital. The John F. Kennedy Stadium was historical, and so was the football rivalry between the two teams. It was a great first day to start our new life in our military adventure. That evening, we met our new neighbors in the renovated family units of the hospital barracks we would be living in for two years. Paul was the only Protestant chaplain on duty, as the Catholic priest was leaving in the next month. Our soon-to-be close friends, six Navy surgeons, and their young families also lived in the barracks. I was excited to be invited to the after-party and to meet the wives in the quarters. Maybe I had been lonelier than I thought as a pastor's wife in Ohio. Our little daughter would have new playmates, and I'd have girlfriends to visit and socialize with, like my friend I had left in Youngstown.

We walked into the unit below us for the party, and a bombshell was quietly and confidentially dropped onto the chaplain after the first round of appetizers were passed. The chilling story of a murdered toddler came tumbling out. She had been found in the garden next to our barracks two weeks prior to our arrival. Nothing could have ever prepared us for this horrific news, and certainly no one wanted to ruin our first day on duty. The doctors and their wives had had to keep their emotions in check for an excruciating two weeks at the barracks and hospital while the crime scene was investigated thoroughly. The new chaplain was just the person they needed to talk with as a collective group. They were grieving and needed a safe place to vent and a mature voice to receive grief support from. We had little to celebrate in the Navy football victory that evening. I was in numbed shock, and so were they. Obviously, this was definitely a life-changer and serious business for the close-knit hospital staff. That evening, we both went to bed with our small daughter between us and hugged each other a little tighter than usual. We quietly wondered if we had made the right decision in leaving Ohio. Were we safe here?

It was a question all seven families would continually ask in the two-year ordeal while living on the gated hospital grounds. We talked about it often and checked windows and doors multiple times during the day and evenings, just in case an intruder had other ideas. I quickly realized I was going crazy with worry; at the time, I did not fully understand the hyper vigilant stress I was under. It was traumatic for us all, but we did have the chaplain, and thank goodness for his grounded wisdom, patience, and mercy in pastoral therapeutic counseling.

It is a strange thing to admit, but at the time, I had

never thought of counseling for myself. Psychology and therapy were not household remedies or luxuries the average person might have benefited from in talking through issues with these mental health experts in the late 1970s. They were certainly not something my family had ever taken part in or talked about. Maybe that was reserved for others with challenges and problems. We asked ourselves repeatedly what was taking so long to find the criminal who had kidnapped this small child; she had been taken out of her own bed on the first floor of our living quarters in the barracks. Death and dying took on a whole new face of terror from the unsolved murder, while I began to spiral a little out of control with a slow, silent, tortured fear, panic, and the anxiety of the workplace in which we lived.

Memories of the past also flooded back, as I also recalled the near-death of my two younger brothers and the experience of crisis that shrouded each one. I had stuffed these memories away for over two decades, and now they were bubbling up, unsolicited. My one-year-old brother had suffered acute spinal meningitis when I was just turning five. We lived with my grandparents in the city at the time, as my parents had already divorced. I remembered the story circulating in the small kitchen that while the physicians were pronouncing death and shutting down his many tubes, my mother happened to notice a miraculous eyelash flutter.

Years later, my youngest brother would have a freak fall out of the car window while playing in the garage, injuring his tiny neck and cutting off oxygen to his brain. It was all devastatingly traumatic and terrorizing in flashbacks to remember hearing the whispers of death, ambulances, and sirens wailing during those sleepless nights. I realized that walking down the hallways of the hospital to visit the sick patients with the chaplain by my side could elicit breathing problems, sweating, and a racing heartbeat. *What in the world was wrong with me?* I feverishly thought to myself. I had neither solution nor answer for these intense, obsessive symptoms or patterns provoke just a stroll. Actually, I cannot even tell you if stress, extreme anxiety, and panic attacks were common in the mental health fields at the time, but it was a malady that could bubble to the surface unpredictably for me.

The Philadelphia Naval Hospital was the East Coast treatment center for our brave and courageous military personnel severely wounded and maimed in the Vietnam War. While walking the ramps into the west wing of the hospital, I could actually smell the death of limbs and of tortured souls. It was perplexing how I could feel the overwhelming sadness and grief permeating the empty corridors where quadriplegics and amputees came for acute care and prosthesis. In conversation with staff, I was also told that these same hallways were used for wheelchair races. *At least there was some levity amongst the broken troops*, I thought.

Was I imagining all this ghostly emotion I literally could taste? I tried to take detours to avoid these corridors, but the yellow military barracks we lived in and the long quadriplegic ramps were in front of the chapel where Paul held services. They were impossible to avoid. Each Sunday, I'd stuff the haunting fear that would grip my throat and hold my breath to run to chapel with our little daughter in my arms. I was deeply bothered by the images of these young men, who sacrificed limb and body for the freedoms many segments of society took so lightly. The awful loss and unsolved murder of a precious child played unmerciful games with my mind.

However, I had new business to focus on, which was a new baby boy. Our beautiful son was born in May, which is a perfectly wonderful month of the year to be born. Spring flowers were up, green grass was appearing, and it was Mother's Day. It was a season of a new birth and the rebirth of Easter. We were all adjusting to our family of four when new orders arrived for ship duty in Japan.

Time to Reflect

1. What fears do you struggle with? Make a list.
2. How can you release them to God and replace them with His love and healing power?

Scripture Study

1. Read 1 John 4:18. Can you trust God to flush out your fears?
2. Read 2 Timothy 1:7. What does God want for you, according to this passage?

Chapter 3

Unspeakable Grief

Humpty Dumpty sat on a wall, Humpty Dumpty had a great fall, all the king's horses and all the king's men could not put Humpty's mother together again.

—*Children's nursery rhyme, with a twist*

The Midway Battle Group

I was not expecting a duty station so far from Texas and my family. Reading through the overseas duty papers with Paul made me a little nervous to find that we would be moving to Japan to live. It was the first time in my life to live away from everything I knew as familiar. During the two months we had to get ready to leave, there were many individuals outside of the military who had plenty to remind me of regarding the Japanese nation and, of course, Pearl Harbor. I detected bitterness and unresolved pain that World War II conjured up in our conversations, so I made it a point to remember this in the foreign country if it was brought up. The movers put half of our personal items in storage while the toys, a few clothes, and several pieces of furniture we needed were shipped to the Far East.

In late December, we left for Japan, where Paul was assigned to the Midway Battle Group on a CG-24 guided-missile cruiser. To say it was a difficult time to arrive in the cold, overcast, and rainy winter month of December would be an understatement. It was definitely a cultural and financial shock to anyone arriving here for the first time. Women with sweet baby-faced children tied to their backs still wore kimonos on the streets; only a handful of brazen teens wore the new Western-styled jeans. Taxi drivers were the most fascinating to observe, as they wore crisp white gloves and uniforms with odd-shaped hats to drive in. They also turned their car lights off at red lights so as not to offend the driver in front. What a nice custom America could use.

The Japanese stores were full of fruits and candies of every flavor, color, and creative shape, but the sticker shock came when I saw a bin of cantaloupes that each sold for a whopping eighty-five dollars. What? That that was $84.25 more than one would pay at a produce stand on Highway 6 in Texas, where I grew up. I was so homesick for Texas, and it had only been a few days since leaving.

My heart sank as the reality of sea duty began to settle in. The Naval base was a massive enclave for the busy fleet while the ships lined up for the Pacific tours looked like long, gray monsters. I gulped several times as we drove up to the USS *Reeves*, which was home ported in Yokosuka. This would be our new home for the next three years. I was nervous and scared, and once again found it hard to catch my breath; I worried about this new life and experienced the same sensation in my throat and breathing that I had while in Philadelphia. I did not want Paul to be concerned, so I kept a stiff upper lip and smiled through the enormous haunting fear of abandonment, which seemed to grip my chest at the most inopportune times.

Paul had to meet the ship two days after arrival, so I was left alone to manage a new life in a foreign country that I wasn't sure I even wanted to be in. I promised myself that I would learn all I could about this odd place in the Far East. It was not the moon, but it was not Kansas, either, although I could have seriously taken Kansas at the time. There was nothing available on the Naval base for dependent housing, so we were instructed that our accommodations would be a Japanese *riokan*, a small hotel in town. With the two small children under tow, my heart sank as I walked through the petite front portico on the main street of Yokosuka.

I perceived the *mama-san* (Japanese name for an austere little woman in charge of the wooden hotel) did not like American women at all, nor did she know how to speak English. She checked me in with many hand gestures and an unkind and stern look that I had not

49

expected. Had I not professed several months before that a family adventure would be awesome in a foreign country? Instead, this is what I got: a real adventure, all right. I felt a wave of nostalgia hit me again for family and my former life. I dared not show vulnerability to this little woman behind the desk, nor to the two children snuggling against my body. It was a sobering wake-up call at twenty-eight years old to face the current reality without someone who cared or could understand the emotional upheaval going on inside of me.

Unfortunately, I was rendered helpless the next morning when the mama-san turned off the heat, after the civilian ship contractors left for work. Did I mention we were freezing not only because of the weather in December, but because the windows of this ancient structure had been built with rice paper? These people were living in the Dark Ages, I thought. Not even glass windows to keep out the damp cold. The three of us were hungry for American food and a few US luxuries (like beds and heat), and here I was, alone with two little ones and morning sickness with our third child. My only friends at the moment in this new Asian environment were Paul II, our six-month-old toddler, and Tara, my three-year-old champ of a daughter. We locked eyes on one another, and I vowed to protect and shield them. I hoped they could see strength and not weakness behind the hazel eyes called "Mom."

Nothing I could think of at the present moment filled the gaping holes of the pity party I was silently throwing for myself. There was not a thing I was grateful for or positive about; I could not see through the situation I was in. We missed our rock of Gibraltar, Dad. I missed the stage and thought how void I felt without my music to fill the gaping holes in my soul. For what it's worth, I also missed my glamorous lifestyle. How sickening was that regretful thought? Here I was, stuck in a foreign country I did not like, freezing in a barn they called a Japanese hotel, pregnant, and with two small children in tow, while unable to provide any resemblance of a home. I missed Mexican food, avocadoes to be exact, the sweet juice of watermelon running down my chin, and my big family back in Texas.

Have you ever made excuses and looked yourself in a mirror while echoing the "why me" of life? It struck me one day that I might be headed in the wrong direction. To be honest, I was on cruise control with God, and for that blaring exclusion of the Almighty Himself, I have absolutely no reason to give you in thinking through this season of my life. I had nothing that I needed from Him or thought He might need from me. Incredulous, you might say. Yes, I was incredibly sad, reflecting on those years without His power in my life. How I could have managed it all without a kind and loving God to draw on for strength, understanding, communication, or direction eludes me. I must have assumed that He was just too busy with people elsewhere. What would He have cared about my situation, anyway? My survival kit of spiritual skill was totally limited and did not include a prayer life nor a Bible, which was on a tanker somewhere between San Francisco and Japan. I had had no training in persevering with God. I did, however, remember to sing the Jesus song each night for Tara and Paul, as we snuggled to keep warm on the Japanese tatami bed, which was laid out on the rice floor. Ha. Would my friends have even believed Rivers was sleeping on a rice mat, of all things? Hopefully, the children believed that Jesus and their mom loved them more than life, which was my only positive thought I could give them.

Much to my delight, we only had to endure the wooden box under the watchful eye of the mama-san for another month. We were transferred to the Navy motel and told we were on the list for base housing in five months. What? Five months. My heart sank at the news of this current predicament. I did not sign up for motel living and would have been perfectly happy to stay in Texas with my family until a home was available. Our small shipment was due in port any day with everything we owned, and it would be five months before the children had their own beds to sleep in and their favorite toys to play with.

The Navy Lodge Motel was a dump with old worn carpet, two beds, and a small disgusting bathroom. I hate to sound so negative and critical of the military, but it was a nightmare to live in for long periods of transitional time. It was exactly what it was supposed to be: a cheap motel for one or two temporary nights for military personnel flying in or out of Japan or headed north as Marines. I think I have seen better accommodations on the mission fields of India and Africa than what we had to live in for one hundred and sixty days. Emotionally and physically, it was a struggle to manage two young children in the dismal room for any length of time, with no kitchen and no car. Good health evaded us during this time, as our baby son had a Japanese flu, which turned out to be chronic; he had to be hospitalized for nineteen ear infections, which required ear tubes, and I endured a gallbladder attack while pregnant. I hope to goodness something has changed in our current military situations for families.

What was most shocking at this Navy Lodge was that there was no phone connection from our room to the front desk, which was located across the road on base. How could they run such an unsafe and unprofessional organization like this with women and dependents living in such squalid conditions? My closest friend at the time was a fighter pilot's wife, who lived in the next room with four small children of her own. She was also waiting for five months for a three-bedroom house. However, we devised our own simple communication system, a form of Morse code, in case of emergency. Each knock on the wall had a number we assigned to it, if we needed a hand or wanted to step outside to just sit and talk while the children slept at night. Definitely, we were improvising a bit of the Dark Ages and trying to solve problems in 1980. I often wished I had memorized that Morse code more closely in the Girl Scouts.

One weekend shortly after meeting, we were both

traumatized and paralyzed with fear when the Fuji Marines came to town and rented out rooms at the Navy motel. They were drunk and tried breaking our doors right off the hinges in their inebriated stupors. We thought we were going to be raped and pillaged and the children killed. Our knocks were fast and furious as we silently screamed for one another's safety. We were both concerned with the effects of this for the six children and for our own mental health.

After that weekend episode, we vowed to change some kind of rule, insisting that phone lines be put in the rooms for the dependent's safety. In civilian life, the request would have been a no-brainer, but we were put on report with our perspective ships as "troublemakers." We were soon to learn as dependent wives that it took Herculean efforts to change military thinking for something so small. Today, I would be standing on my head in the fleet admiral's office instead of meekly trying to placate some motel worker at the front desk. During this deployment, I was additionally going to be educated in assertiveness training and learn what *hutzpah* meant and what it could do when applied for in courage.

Upon arrival in Japan as dependents, we were required to take a cultural course. It was an extremely fascinating course on Eastern culture and protocol, and the Navy instructors recommended three things: First, we should learn the language as quickly as possible. Ha! Have you ever seen the Japanese kanji figures? Although I considered myself to be fairly optimistic in my twenties, it would be a miraculous feat to conquer the language with thousands of these figures written in thick black scrolls. The Japanese counting system alone used three different methods. To this first instruction, I reminded myself that Rome was not built in a day; always a good student, I adapted to the language barrier by using hand signals while keeping a pad and pencil in my purse to draw maps and figures. I relied heavily on our little daughter to understand what was being communicated. Kids are so smart. Tara picked up the complex dialect much faster than I.

Second, we were instructed that we needed to study the culture to become great hostesses for those who would be visiting from the States. To this second and somewhat lame imperative, I quickly ascertained no one would want to travel from America to visit, so it took me off the hook for this request, although after some time of living in the culture, it would have been a lovely place to play tour guide for. Lastly, the instructors told us to never get too sick on a weekend and need a Japanese hospital. The reasons were multifaceted, but I mentally checked the invisible box and emphasized "never on a Saturday or Sunday," written in my notes.

It was September, and I was one month shy of turning thirty when our third child was born. The ship's captain allowed Paul to remain in port for her overdue birth for three days and then gave him permission to fly out to meet the battle group in the Asian Pacific theatre. We had moved into base housing two weeks prior to her birth, after waiting eight months in the Navy Lodge. I had not had time to prepare and assess each room for safety, as it was so hectic in the move-in with a newborn, a toddler, and a four-year-old. As most pregnancies and post-delivery go, I also had no sleep in the last six weeks and was panicking to think of all the things I needed to do to be organized, ready, and awake in order to face anything with three small children. I was quickly becoming overwhelmed as a single mother with a husband out to sea and without any fixed schedules or routines. I was learning to survive at twenty-nine years old.

September 10, 1981

What started out as a typical afternoon soon turned into sheer terror, in a chain of events that forever changed our lives as individuals, a couple, and a family. After feeding my nine-day-old, I laid her down and remember going into the kitchen to start dinner when I heard the loud thud. In the confusion to follow, I thought the paperboy might be delivering early and had slammed the rolled newspaper into the front door. I turned and rushed back into the next room, where the newborn was screaming for a diaper change. I soon realized in seconds that our sixteen-month-old, Paul II, was nowhere to be seen in the small downstairs apartment and must have started up the stairs to investigate on his own for the first time. But it was the panic alert button that sounded when Tara announced in a loud voice from the sidewalk outside that her brother had fallen out of the window. The thud. I remember the words and her sweet little voice as if they were spoken yesterday: "Mommy, baby Paul fell out of the window." Time seemed to stop, as I stood frozen in my footsteps. I ran down the narrow hallway but collapsed two feet from the front door. I remembered. It was a Saturday.

The hospital staff quickly ushered me into a small room close to the emergency room, where they had rushed our baby son. Many readers will understand the battle of emotions in an emergency trauma situation. I sat in numbed shock in the sterile space, trying to recall any details. Four walls would become my friend and foe in a matter of minutes, as I would have been perfectly happy to die on the spot from the suffocating pain. A neighbor must have called the ambulance because several people rushed to our house to care for Jordan and Tara. I would have gladly exchanged the last hour with anyone on planet earth, but no one would have volunteered for the living hell of it all. It is said that death has many faces. I saw them all as life ebbed out of the small toddler next door to me.

The human emotions that come with unspeakable grief are a cruel reminder that life is fleeting, as we deal with a traumatic life-changing event. First, the disbelief and shock settled in as I sat helplessly in that small, sterile room, looking at a black hole somewhere in my mind. I wanted to desperately wake up from this horrific nightmare and just have it all go away. I gave myself a whopping F for failure as a mother, a protector, and a lifesaver. What could I possibly do to unravel the last hour? How was I going to live? How was I going to make it through this ordeal if my child died? How was I going to make it without him? His cute little smile, his chunky little legs, his snuggly hugs. I hated myself. Why were we sent to this place? Why did I travel here? I started to rehearse these conversations and questions with God, hoping at the time He might hear me, if He was even there. That window, that rotten stinking window was unsafe, missing a screen on one side. I hated it too. Why had I not seen the impending danger before?

My mind began playing sick games as each new physician's prognosis of the little life in the emergency room became more severe. I could think of nothing more than the harshest punishment I deserved for killing my child, if he died. The screams from my body would not disappear. I made a last-ditch effort in a passionate plea for mercy and bargained for his little life, praying that God might save him. I begged and told Him that I would give up the one thing I loved to do, which was to sing. To be honest with you, it was the only thing I thought He might want to hear from me. "If you save Paul, I will never sing again. I will never go on stage again nor have the desire for that life." It was all I knew to do at the time. I was young, and it must have sounded shallow, but I was being totally honest with God. At the moment, it was the only concrete solution I had.

Because of the severity of the head trauma, the medical team told me Paul was now in grave condition; they did not believe he would make it through the night. If he did, he would probably remain in a vegetative state. The attending physicians thought there was not enough time for the medical flight to get him to the Philippines. He was in need of life-saving surgery to relieve the pressure on his brain. There was no option for me to back out from my deal with God. My heart sank. I prayed feebly and screamed out louder for mercy for the first time in my whole adult life. I screamed and screamed that night for God to come and save him, to do something to give me hope.

Life as I knew it came to an abrupt halt. It was not what I was prepared for as a young mother of a four-year-old, a sixteen-month-old, and a nine-day-old. Medically, every minute counted for him. The team was going to have to act quickly, they said. The ambulance was ordered to take him to the Japanese hospital for a CAT scan, and I was told to go home.

It was still Saturday. I died a million deaths waiting by the phone. Degrees of looking death in the face are frightening and can come with unchartered territory for any one of us going through an ordeal like this. Unless one is a first responder to crisis or a seasoned warrior, the human brain is not equipped to handle sudden death or catastrophic trauma. A dreadful sense of foreboding doom washed over me as I began the descent into what I will call my dark night of the soul. It would last for over twenty years, until I received qualified help.

Days later, I was able to give my mind permission

to think through the last forty-eight hours. I somehow remembered to thank God that He had sent four men and a woman to miraculously help our little son on September 10. First, there was a multilingual Chinese Japanese-speaking Navy pediatrician to thank, who had been on ER duty that day at the Naval hospital. Second, there was a young Japanese neurosurgeon from Tokyo who had come by train at the urgent ER call. I would later find out he had also studied pediatric neurology in America. Third, a loving Nazarene chaplain, Dudley Hathaway, had come to hold my hand through all of those grueling hours of waiting in the sterile hospital room. Lastly, God had provided a wonderful communications captain, who was in charge of coded radio transmissions throughout Asia, and his loving, Spirit-led wife. The captain sent a six-word communiqué to Paul, who was in the Indian Ocean on top-secret maneuvers. It read "Son gravely injured, proceed home immediately." Those were the only words that Paul had for four days as he traveled from the battle group to reach Yokosuka Naval Hospital. It took years for me to discuss it in length with him, but it must have been heart stopping for him to have to bear that message with so little to go on.

The godly captain's wife rode in the ambulance to the Japanese hospital and prayed for Paul like the saint she was. She was God's healing arm that night, as she prayed over him in the ambulance and during the CAT scan. Because our small Paul was clinging to life in a coma and the brain swelling was so severe, I was not allowed to touch him or tell him I was there in ICU when he returned. When they ushered me into the sacrosanct wing of the hospital, I was only allowed a two-minute visit. I remember his heart rate was racing at an astronomical number over number on the monitors.

Tubes were everywhere. I hated hospitals. The ICU staff warned that the brain was trying to get the oxygen it needed for repair and not to be shocked when I saw him. His head had swollen to ten times its normal size. If the ICU floor had opened, I would have gladly let it swallow me. I was driven home that night, a broken woman thinking the life had been sucked out of me and feeling as if I was a hundred years old. The thought of our son not knowing I was there to speak love over him haunted me for many years.

It would take years of recovery in physical rehabilitation for him, as God did in fact save his life, and it would take almost twenty-three years for his mother to be put back together again. His issue was life. Hers was about asking to be reborn into life. His injury was diagnosed as an acute traumatic brain injury (TBI); hers would not be diagnosed until much later. It would be coined as post-traumatic stress syndrome (PTSD) when it was finally identified. Simply defined, it's the reenactment of a traumatizing event repetitively, but obsessively trying to change the outcome. That described me in a nutshell.

There was nothing I could do to change the outcome of the accident that day. As with any tragic accident, no one can rewind history. Sadly, if the medical community had

had a medical term for this syndrome in the early 1980s, I possibly could have received care and help much earlier for my child and myself and our family. My unresolved issues took deeper root into self-rejection and disgust for letting this accident happen on my watch. The blame was not going to be about punishing bad or good behavior; however, it was going to debilitate me, as I held myself accountable for every aspect of our son's recovery and his life thereafter. I fought almost to the death to pull myself through paralyzing anxiety and fears that eventually turned to phobias. My symptoms mirrored a Civil War reenactment going on, but the battlefield was in my mind.

Meticulously, I could recall every detail of sound, every conversation, and every action that was taken or not taken. I rehearsed different scenarios each day and lay in bed at night, waiting for the night terrors to begin. The only ray of hope during those early months of Paul's recovery was a story that landed on the front page of the *Navy Times* in Japan about a baseball pitcher, Tommy John. His two-year-old had fallen out of a third-floor window at about the same time. My hope was built around his surviving a seventeen-day coma. One day, I would like to talk with Tommy John and his wife. I could tell them how impactful their story was; I read every word in the paper that was reported through his recovery. I also received three letters from America from former military families whose children had had near misses out of those unsafe windows. They guiltily wrote they should have vigorously pursued the safety issue of the windows with the Navy Base Housing Office. I wish they had done that too.

I want to close this chapter out for anyone who might need a touch from God today. Your story is as unique as your fingerprints. I understand what you are going through, and although I don't know your name or circumstance, I do know the anguish in your heart and the gut-wrenching pain you might have endured. I understand it all. It would take years for me to finally let go and let the Holy Spirit come to my rescue when I needed it the most to comfort me. Was God for real? Did He exist? Did He even care? I would have to find answers to these questions. What was I even on earth to do, anyway? This was the quest that I was on: to find peace and trust. I would need the strength and love from above to give to my children and husband, and to grasp what unspeakable grief does to one who cannot forget. It was going to be the path of healing that God would use to bring the broken to me in the end.

Of course, never doubt it: God loves healing, and yes, if I could, I'd have rewritten a new script for those lost years of Paul's life and the emotional time our entire family went through. I would have done anything to have a different outcome. God would have Paul in His gentle arms and care. We firmly believed our children had been given to God in Holy Baptism, covered by the blood of the Lamb to eventually live their own inspired and purpose-driven lives.

Love will conquer all. It covers fears, phobias, anxiety,

and stress. It heals the deepest of heartbreak and scars that run deep. I believe those who persevere will have a victory to share. The grief that I had to overcome became my banner to fight the evil one, in the name of Jesus. I could only do this in the power of the Spirit. The thief who had stolen the health of my child, had stolen the peace of our little family, had stolen my voice and nearly my soul gave me the impetus to learn how to stand strong in the face of trial with that backbone of steel to stay the course.

The sign would come, the visions and dreams would begin, and they would bring the healing salve of Jesus. If you allow God, you will have the victory at the end yourself. He will never abandon you or forsake you. I can make this promise, if you are willing to take His hand. He was the King Who had to put me back together again and break through the walls I had built around my heart. He was also the King Who walked me out of the darkness into the light as a renewed and born-again woman. You will read about the miraculous work He would do, but it would still take a road less traveled to get to the eventual truth I had to recognize: that God would never test me beyond the faith to handle it. It was the faith part that was tricky for me to confront, but thank God, He sent His Son to save me, and thank God He sent His Spirit to comfort me and give me the courage to live. In living, I was going to be able to help others live. This story is about to unfold for you, as the doors slowly open to miraculous healing.

Time to Reflect

1. Have you ever experienced a traumatic loss and tried to bargain with God?
2. How were you able to work through your grief and your loss with God's help?

Scripture Study

1. Read Romans 8:28. Do you think God will work good out of everything if you love Him?
2. Read Romans 8:38–39. Can anything separate you from God?

Chapter 4

A Rabbi and the White Scarf

In 1982, we left Japan and landed on the West Coast for our new military orders. I was grateful to be back in Western civilization and enjoyed the familiarity of American life in the beautiful coastal city of San Francisco. Paul worked for the chief of chaplains as a recruiter for the eleven Western states, traveling during the week and thankfully returning home on the weekends. During this time, I was in an exhaustive survival mode during the week while he was away. Because of our son's accident in Japan, neither one of us realized the impact of what was going on physically or emotionally. I rarely slept except in a chair in our living room with the drapes open. I let the two girls sleep in our bed on many nights so they could be close to me in the next room, while Paul II slept on a Japanese tatami on the floor in the second bedroom. I thought if there was any danger, a passerby on the street might hear my cries for help and assist me. The open drapes became my security blanket, as strange as that sounds, but the habit helped soothe anxiety and fear.

It was not until early 2000 that research studies of returning wounded veterans from Desert Storm, Iraq, and Afghanistan revealed how severe TBI and PTSD could affect one's mental health. Physicians soon realized that veterans suffering from PTSD had coping mechanisms critical to their survival. My survival tactic happened to be open drapes and sleeping in a chair, which of course helped foster the panic and hypervigilant stance. My symptoms also worsened with each steep hill I had to drive on in San Francisco and navigating the two massive bridges: San Francisco Bay and the Oakland Bay Bridges. I am sure it did not help my stability in having to drive a Volkswagen with stick shift on these steep inclines and bridges. I had severe nausea, my palms became sweaty, and I could hardly breathe. The signs of PTSD were not yet familiar until the reports and research continued to mount during Desert Storm.

I have skipped ahead of myself in talking about PTSD, but I was getting our San Francisco row house on Thirty-Sixth Avenue organized and livable when the news flashed one morning that a little boy named Adam Walsh had been abducted. The nation was instantly on high alert for its children, and I became obsessive over our three. The search for Adam was agonizing and intensely personal for me, and while I had never met this family, the pain of loss was real and too close for comfort in handling their crisis from a television screen. Every news report and detail about the kidnapping became crucial to watch and filter, as if any ray of hope might be unearthed for this little boy. I wanted his return to be victorious for his parents so I could participate in their celebration. In California, signs and posters were plastered along the streets, toll plazas, and highways. I knew the dread his parents were experiencing and had to believe that this child was going to be found safe and unharmed. That would not be the case, but his parents never stopped believing or searching. Nor did I. Our children never left my sight, except for school. Was my faith weak? The vigilance was maddening.

A few months later, during a dinner party we hosted, I confessed the entire ordeal of the last few years to a young rabbi who served in the Navy chaplaincy with Paul. To my utter surprise, he gently explained about phobias and said I had a phobia, not weak faith. I was not being punished by a judging God? What? A phobia. I suddenly felt reassured with having a prognosis like a phobia. I had never heard this medical term before, but I felt relieved knowing a name had been identified with my situation.

Little did I know that he and Paul had also conspired that evening to get me a dog, as dogs and phobias somehow were compatible. Go figure. He believed a dog would help me feel more secure and in control if a panic attack ensued.

I politely said, "No, thank you, not another thing to be responsible for or feed." I had nursery school car pools, meals, appointments, schedules, and housekeeping to think about. I did not need one more thing to have hanging around. But the very next weekend, the front door opened, and in walked all three children and a dad who proudly presented me with Zeus, the ugliest rescued Dalmatian I had ever seen. I felt bad for the rescued animal. She had too many black spots and a name I did not like. Where had they found this homely thing?

Thankfully, I would not hold my newest companion guilty for too long. I soon found the friend was just what Dr. Rabbi had ordered and also found that Zeus was my angel dog. She was a gift that I loved for the next eight years while dealing with panic attacks. Through investigative research on the syndrome, I learned that extreme anxiety could produce "future-oriented catastrophic thinking," or more easily defined as fear of the future. Yes, panic attacks could suddenly appear without warning, but I had Zeus by my side; I also relied on breathing techniques I learned in childbirth classes and calmed my nerves by praying the Lord's Prayer. Admittedly, I still struggle when I see a child around high windows or stair railings.

The White Scarf

You may not know this, but God often uses us for His purposes when we absolutely have no idea we are working in concert with His plan. God was definitely working in the life of an elderly Jewish man who lived down the street. His name was Sol. I remembered this fabulous little story while writing the previous chapter to illustrate how God speaks to us, even when we are totally unaware that we are listening to His voice. Remember:

I was a true novice, and God often uses the foolish to confound the wise. I marveled once again how the infinite God works His own timeline out. I think you might enjoy reading about Sol and how a lovely Saturday must have turned his world upside down.

One weekend soon after moving from Japan, we had a giant tag sale on the busy boulevard in front of our small driveway. We lived in the Sunset area of San Francisco on Thirty-Sixth Avenue and hoped to unload much of what had been in storage while living in Japan. Late that Saturday afternoon, we were about to end the sale when an elderly man timidly approached our tables. He introduced himself, and in a short, friendly conversation, we learned he lived alone in the next block and had been a widower for over twenty years.

I asked him if there was anything in particular he was looking for. He quickly assessed our tables and muttered we probably did not have what he was looking for. I thought for a moment and told him to stay put while I excitedly ran up the stairs to Paul's dresser.

At the time, I had no earthly idea what prompted me to know what I wanted to give him as a gift, but rummaging through one of Paul's military drawers, I found exactly what I was looking for. Paul had a beautiful white silk scarf that he wore with his wool overcoat for dressy Naval affairs. I did not think twice about giving away one of his fine-looking accessories and hoped he would not mind. I quickly pulled it out of the drawer, refolded it meticulously, and ran back to Sol, who had waited for me on the sidewalk.

When I handed him the scarf, his face went ashen white, almost as white as the silk. He wanted to pay for it, but I explained it was a gift and wanted nothing for it. It was his. He quickly left with a wave of his hand. If he had been a little younger, I think he would have sprinted home, as he seemed to be in shock and somewhat dazed. I thought it might have been about receiving a gift from a total stranger, but the next afternoon, he came back to explain what had happened. It was a lovely reminder that God knows exactly what He is doing at all times and in all ways. God will be God, well, because He is God.

Sol's Sign

Sol shared that he had become friends with a nurse in the hospital he had met during his wife's illness. After his wife died, she had invited him to church many times, but he would politely turn her down because he was Jewish. However, their friendship grew, and she always shared her Christian faith, and they often talked about God and his Orthodox faith. Ultimately, the conversations always turned to eternal life and the Messiah. That Saturday morning of my tag sale, he had awakened to talk to God once and for all to settle the issue of the Messiah that the kind nurse had spoken so much about. He needed his mind to be at peace in order to function, and he could not achieve this without resolving this one last issue. If this

Jewish Messiah was indeed for real and had died for him on the Cross, then he needed a sign from God.

He had told God that very morning he would accept this Jesus Messiah if he found a white scarf that very day. Little did he think anything like a white scarf would appear as the sign he needed. He did not have a car to even go shopping. You can imagine the utter shock when I ran down my steps and laid the beautiful silk gift in his shaking hands. Hallelujah for God, right? What a priceless sign to confirm a man's quest for eternal life and his Messiah, using a tag sale and an unsuspecting actor like me in the story.

Our family became very good friends with Sol after that day, even attending services at his temple. I know without a doubt we will see Sol in heaven, totally because of a white scarf.

Life kept me busy with three small children in the city and a beautiful coastline to explore. I think the natural beauty of California was a tonic that helped all of us to heal. The weekends became our special family time to explore the coastal towns, ski the mountains, and spend countless hours winding through the valleys of Marin County. We especially enjoyed living near the exciting new Lucas Studios in San Rafael. As a fun story to share with readers, *Star Wars* had just exploded on the scene, and we were often treated to our favorite characters roaming through the new Nordstrom's that had opened in the shopping center nearby. Only in California could one run into movie characters in a shopping center. The children were ecstatic, as was their mother.

Over the next three years, several Bay Area churches fell in love with Paul's high standards of ministry, mentoring, and preaching; several tried to persuade him to accept the call as their senior pastor. But we had accepted our next assignment and mentally had moved on to our next post, on the East Coast. Did I mention I was still on cruise control with God?

Academy Life

Orders had arrived for us to transfer to the well-heeled military lifestyle of college academia, training aspiring young cadets to be future officers. This transfer actually enabled our family to have additional time of rest and restoration; it was fun to be with young college students who loved to be with our children and with their "Chaps," as they called him. We soon found that academy life was not as harried as hospital chaplaincy, sea duty, or recruiting, although Chaps did a lot of counseling. I am pretty sure the actual amount of tissues he ordered for the chapel program was high, as they were used for all of those hours sitting across homesick, heartsick, and discouraged students. God was giving us a treasure trove of fond memories and stability, which was wonderful for our health.

After two and half years, we nervously looked forward to Paul's next military move, to an elite group of fighting Marines in Quantico, Virginia. His career was soaring and meticulously mapped out politically by those in Washington. He was on top of his career path, and we knew the next four or five tours would be an even greater challenge for us as a Navy family. These were longer deployments in war-torn areas with the Marines, training alongside soldiers in urban, jungle, and desert warfare, and subsequently senior management of the Chaplain Corps. We had proudly and faithfully served our country, but when the official papers arrived for duty change, another set of papers was also in the mail. As I reflected years later on those papers, I am sure they were from God. While we were in the midst of college and cadets, I started a small business as an entrepreneur that soon grew to be a very successful apparel manufacturing company, which took me back to Asia and the Far East for production. I don't know if I'd have started it had I known all the pitfalls that overseas production brought to a growing business. I won't write about all that happened, but seven good years turned into thirty-three years of headaches and heartbreaking reality, professionally and personally.

The St. Paul Lutheran Church Call Committee from Westport, Connecticut, formally invited Paul to become the next full-time senior pastor of the church. He decided to visit and help the leadership of the church process their due diligence, intending to politely say, "Thank you, but no thanks, our calling is with the military." I was certain that he had told them so.

To my astonishment, he returned from the second consulting meeting and said he was seriously considering the ministerial call to Westport. It must have been an agonizing decision to leave the successful Navy career he loved so much. He was a great leader and commander, now in the Chaplain Corps: always loyal, faithful, wise, and a man of integrity. He was also an awesome father who wanted to see his children grow up, but not from the deck of a ship or a bunker in the deserts of Afghanistan. After following this man around the world and clocking the emotional mileage we now had in the military, I agreed with him. Maybe it was time for roots and a church we could call home. I was looking for family and hoped I might find it sooner than later.

After prayerful consideration and sad farewells, we began what seemed a more stable life for our family in Fairfield County, Connecticut. Normal might have seemed short-lived for us; one sunny afternoon in 1994, on a teaching assignment from the War College in Newport, Rhode Island, the Holy Spirit interrupted my husband's life in a most dramatic, unsolicited, and powerful experience. I was in shock as I listened to him disclose the entire experience. Here are some of the details in this puzzling mystery of the Holy Spirit and what transpired that day.

Paul's Encounter with God

In 1994, the Navy Chaplain Corps asked Paul to give a presentation on ethics and morality in the military to the Naval War College. When he arrived in Newport, Rhode Island, he met Allan, an old acquaintance he had not seen in fifteen years. He was taken aback when Allan made the startling statement that he knew Paul would be coming that morning. He claimed that while in worship a few days earlier, the Lord had told him all that would transpire.

This strange declaration caught Paul totally off-guard for a moment, but he arranged to meet his friend later for a time of prayer and lunch. He was also anxious to hear his friend's story of the dramatic spiritual change that had taken place several years earlier in his life.

Later that afternoon, they met and prayed in Allan's office; his friend made two significant petitions that penetrated Paul's heart. First, he exhorted God to take the burden of control from Paul's shoulders. This touched off an unexpected, uncontrollable firestorm of emotion. Showing personal emotion was something Paul Teske never did in public.

His second petition in prayer was that God would give Paul the patience to wait on His timing. They prayed for a while longer, went to lunch, and bid one another farewell after a lengthy discussion of the spiritual aspects the Holy Spirit brings to an individual's life. While driving home, he headed south on I-95 and began to pray. He explained to me later that these prayers seemed to flow into a time of weeping and song, without regard to content or context. He heard himself speaking incoherently, like a foreign language. He tried to stop but found he had no control over sounds and would switch back to English for a short period, then back to what seemed like gibberish. He felt confounded, confused, and out of control, while anxiety rose just short of panic.

Paul was not a man to be out of control in any aspect of his life. It took more than a few miles to realize that whatever this was, it was not going to subside. He continued to wrestle with his own will to manage the situation but found that he could not stop the cadence of shifting back and forth. He thought he might be losing his mind. If this was from God, he thought, then He was going to have to convince him with a remarkable sign. He suggested that God show him the number 5. He looked up and saw that he was quickly approaching Exit 55 on I-95 and saw milepost 55, and the speed was even 55 mph. This seemed too subliminal, so he asked for another sign: "Lord, if this is all really from you, let the next car that passes have a 2 in the license plate." (License plates in Connecticut consisted of three numbers and three letters.) He slowed down, and the next car that passed him had three 2s in the license plate: 222. This all overwhelmed him, and he began to praise God, both because he knew that the strange sounds erupting from his mouth were the tongues of praise initiated by the Holy Spirit and that God had indeed given him a miraculous sign of confirmation.

He later shared that he wept, laughed, and felt an incredible joy over his entire being, but anxiety returned as his thoughts shifted to what awaited him in Westport: me. A traditional Lutheran church with several hundred members and an ex-independent Baptist wife, none of whom believed in this stuff. He said his joy slowly dissipated, and his mind was flooded with worry and concern. He knew that what he had just received was real, and also knew with the same degree of certainty that the battleground ahead would be difficult. What was he going to do with all of this? Why had God chosen that very day?

Paul moved quite well in his own strength and power, but now he sensed the power of God was going to overcome anything he had previously brought to the equation. He knew that the greatest test of his life rested at the end of the drive home. He did not know it in that moment, but he later came to realize that God would have His way in His own timing.

Rivers' Perspective

Paul walked into the house from the War College, and I was excited to hear about our old life and any of our friends in the Navy he might have seen.

But what he asked me immediately in the conversation took me off-guard: "Hey, do I look different to you?"

Well, Paul would never have asked me such a question. He was always confident about his looks and would never have started a conversation in such an unusual way. I was a little taken aback and incredulous as his story unfolded about seeing our old friend and what had just taken place on the highway. He was a little nervous as he rapidly detailed what had happened after leaving the War College.

I remember saying something stupid like, "What is God going to think about all of this?"

Believing in all of this Holy Spirit stuff was close to heresy, I thought. I actually had no spiritual lens through which to assess this newly found relationship with God and the entire godhead. So all I knew was confusion and an overwhelming feeling, having been lost in a downward spiral somewhere in his excitement and discussion. For a lifetime in a mainline church and military chaplaincy, I had played it safe at arm's length with God and had liked the status quo, only because I never expected or knew anything different.

Maybe you have been in this same place. Cruise control with God seemed safe enough, and I quite liked it just the way it was. I would eventually recognize that I was going through all the motions from my head but not my heart. I heard the word *miracle* used several times in the next several years but assumed it only applied to Moses's escape from Egypt or Jesus's healings in the New Testament. The funny part about ignorance is that sometimes one is oblivious or unaware to understanding there could be anything more? I knew I wanted more out of life; I wanted to have incredible faith and peace but did not know I was truly lost or missing out on anything. As it so happened, as a pastor's wife, I was really close to drowning in gripping fears, loneliness, guilt, and the list could go on, as I think about the challenges at the time.

Standing here before me was a husband who just had the most far-fetched encounter I ever heard of. What was I going to do with all of this information and uncertainty?

Throughout our marriage, I had always trusted Paul's leadership, guidance, and wisdom, but this peculiar experience of his was unsettling. He had been a Gibraltar rock and solidly on a path that was always reasonable and wise, but this unsolicited, Spirit-led experience in his car made the event even more mysterious and frustrating for me. After my initial question of what God was going to think, I guess God had thought a lot about what He was going to think. It became the greatest struggle of our marriage over the next six years. We fought, I cried, we lost our friends and half of our congregation, and I cried more.

Why? Why was the Holy Spirit so difficult for me to handle? And why did I have to be dragged into all this drama? Our family had been loyal to the end with all of our friends, so it was shocking to me and to the children when friends left the church and left our friendship to dangle over the third person of the Trinity. Probably one of the hardest and most wounding aspects of ministry life is to emotionally let friends go when they make the choice to leave. Most never say goodbye, and that is the emotional heartbreak of struggling with the realities of life in ministry. They just disappear without a goodbye. I still pray through several experiences that left our children deeply wounded. They are forgiven, but we all had to learn many hard lessons in keeping our eyes focused on Jesus and not on humans. The Holy Spirit issue eventually taught us a great lesson, that life can be cruel, but perseverance and overcoming in the strength of the Lord is the only way to endure all that life throws at us, even in ministry dysfunction.

Paul spent many prayerful nights at the healing services he started soon after his encounter. Many times, he sat alone in the sanctuary with God by his side, and his great resolve and tenacious faith strengthened him in this daily walk. After the road trip changed his life, so did the services at church. He disbanded the choir, fired the organist, and purchased an organ that played the greatest hymns of faith on a recorded platform, hired a worship team, hung up his vestments for the second service, and began anointing the sick with oil.

What in the world was he thinking? At the time, I thought the Catholic Church reserved oil for the last rites, so the paradigm shift quickly became contentious. I found myself fighting both God and Paul on so many issues that I became exhausted. Those two were a formidable duo. I could win a few with Paul, but not God, and that was the utterly confusing thing about the entire disruptive spiritual situation. I was battle weary, but Paul thought that a spiritual retreat was what I needed to help me out. I had never been to any kind of retreat, so I went tentatively, expecting something like a spa outing. Ha. For the sequestered weekend, our watches were taken away and phone service was not allowed, unless there was an emergency. Not bad for starters. To my surprise, there were approximately thirty-five women on the retreat, all of whom received cards of encouragement from total strangers in other churches. I had never been so blessed by people I did not know. However, it was an Anglican priest who changed my paradigm by anointing my forehead with oil on the first evening. The dear man made a sign of the Cross on my forehead, called me by name, and then prayed a deeply moving blessing and prayer over me. I had never been anointed by a dab of oil that smelled so rich and pungent. It was a simple prayer, encouraging me to listen attentively to the speakers and ponder the inexplicable peace that had come over me when touched with holy oil on my forehead. I was starting to thaw while cupped in the palm of God's hands.

After returning from the weekend retreat, God was going to show up in a most unbelievable way by using a newborn baby. The bizarre situation would not only get our attention together as a couple but collectively, as a church, a few weeks later. This would be the first foray into Paul's life with the miraculous that I would not be able to question as anything but a Sovereign God, and now my world was rocked.

The next Sunday evening, Paul was called into the maternity ER at a local hospital to pray for one of our congregants, who had had their first baby. The child had been diagnosed with dwarfism and also a syndrome where the organs did not develop normally. The baby only had a few months to live, he was told. Paul could see the extremities and torso, which showed all the signs of dwarfism. In front of the devastated parents and medical staff, Paul took the tiny bundle in his arms and prayed a powerful prayer that ended with, "God, you are going heal this baby completely so he may live a productive and healthy life."

He told me later that he could not believe he was saying these words, even as the prayer came out of his mouth. He said he felt like a jerk to have said something so absurd, knowing the prognosis was grave; the baby was expected to die from this rare syndrome. He also shared that he was afraid to open his eyes, thinking the parents would be livid that he had prayed such a thing regarding their child. He quickly said, "Amen," and left the hospital. In the elevator to the parking lot, he second-guessed himself, wondering if he had indeed said what he thought he had said, since the parents had shown no reaction to the word *heal* or to his prayer.

They took the small newborn to Yale Hospital in New Haven. The mother called Paul several days later; sobbing, she said that the baby was indeed a dwarf but did not have the syndrome. Paul thanked Jesus that the syndrome tests were wrong. He felt a bit better about the prayer of healing he said, but the baby was then transferred to Columbia Hospital in New York City for further tests. Ten days later, he received yet another call from the hysterical mother; he left the office and raced to her house, several blocks away. Now his thought was, *Oh no, the tests were indeed correct, and the baby is going to die.* When he arrived, the young mother was in the yard, talking on a portable phone with the baby in her arms. When she saw him walking toward her, she dropped the phone and ran into his arms.

He began to comfort her and heard her tearfully explain, "Pastor, the baby is not a dwarf and does not have any syndrome."

Paul was shaken to the core, as he remembered every word of his prayer, which he had not believed. He thanked God and gave Him all the glory as he drove back to the church after the miraculous news. He relayed the entire scene to me that evening. I was incredulous and, of course, now had to think of this life-changing healing drama that had taken place so close to home. The news was miraculous, and we rejoiced that a precious newborn had been healed. A new season had begun for Paul, not quite yet for me, but the iceberg was certainly melting.

The Final Argument with God

Going through the fire with God was like climbing a mountain on an iceberg. It was incredibly exhausting, individually and on our marriage, as I have shared. I think our whole family was clinging to the side of the mountain, which sounds dramatic but true. In retrospect, maybe the children were still too young to understand all the dynamics spinning around the situation, but I was either stubborn or had a sack over my head. I have to admit God was relentless, while going for the very soul of our church. Thank You, Jesus, that He believed in us that much, because each new level was a vigorous test with Paul at the helm.

We have a banner that hangs in the front of our church for all to see that says "God Will Make a Way." Countless people, including myself, have said they were hanging on to a fragile hope, in the belief that He was making a way in all circumstances. While the Spirit was breaking down the walls of distrust and helplessness on my part, God the Father was setting up further breakthroughs and another holy tsunamis.

Paul sent me to a second weekend retreat, but this time to a more staid conference in the Billy Graham Center at Wheaton College. I agreed to go, as it sounded totally benign, and who could argue with Billy and Ruth Graham? Paul had heard of Wheaton's Lee Ann Payne and wanted me to learn more about a new inner healing conference she was hosting. I agreed to go with an open mind and listen to the speakers. I had no point of reference for female presenters. Did we even believe in women presenting at this time in the Lutheran church? Hardly.

Lee Ann could have been my grandmother. She spoke with such gentle authority on God and believed that the Kingdom of God had become slothful and an ugly bride for Jesus to be married to. Wow. I had never seen an ugly bride but got the picture and the gravity of the church's problem from her teaching. This grandmother was pulling no punches in her beliefs or her delivery. Her biography on the back of the agenda stated she had been a professor at Wheaton, and I imagined she was a tough academician. She had my undivided attention on the subjects of healing deliverance, which I knew nothing about. Were these exorcisms? She spoke about the importance of the Father's love, practicing His presence, and sharpening our minds in the Word of God. I was captivated by her great knowledge and love of scripture and sat straighter in my seat as she touched on the topic of the Father's love. She was articulate and taught at great length about the poor attitude of the church (I could tell she would not tolerate one second of slovenliness) and reprimanded the pulpits of God for not taking a stand on critical social issues and ills that were destroying society and the fabric of the American church.

She also spoke right to the heart of how women should make their homes beautiful and organized to honor God's provision of a home and a family. I overheard at lunch that she had just had several skylights installed in her home so she could see the beauty of God in the sun and moonlight. Ms. Payne was probably a backyard camper in her youth like me, if she loved to ponder the heavens.

The worship was much different at the conference. I was not familiar with the newer worship style, but people were clapping and raising their hands, which I vowed to never do at the time. I did not want to be conspicuous, which of course I was. Out of the 750 attendees, 749 were raising their hands and singing. Classically trained singers would never do a thing such as raise hands, unless dying on stage or belting out a high note, but then who was I? I had not sung since 1981.

On the second afternoon, prayer teams were lined up along the walls of the giant room. Ms. Payne had instructed attendees if anyone needed prayer, there would be two on each team for us. I had never experienced this type of prayer structure before. I sat frozen in my chair. I could not be so vulnerable with a stranger and surely did not want any secrets to slip out. What if someone found out who I really was and judged me? Nope, I was not going to participate in this exercise.

However, a supernatural force actually held me glued to the chair so forcibly that I had back spasms. Remembering this, I am sure the evil one did not want any kind of beautiful prayer spoken over my life. Whatever the cause, I decided to try and pray on my own. So I sat with my head bowed while a harpist played from the stage. It was glorious and almost celestial, and I closed my eyes. All sound was soon shut out, and I thought I might have fallen asleep. A green light flashed behind my eyes, and then a picture, like a movie, unfolded of Jesus, Who appeared on a mountaintop plateau with me, much like *The Sound of Music*. Spring flowers were scattered throughout the green grass. Who knows, maybe I was truly in Austria with Him.

I saw myself as a small girl with long, blonde pigtails hanging down the back of my blue dress. He was dancing a simple child's dance in circles with me while we held hands. He was laughing and smiling, and my yellow ribbons were flying as we twirled faster. I had not felt happier in my life, and much to my surprise, Jesus giggled with me. His smile made His eyes crinkle. I have no idea how long He and I hung out together on the mountaintop, but when I opened my eyes, the harp was still playing a soft prayerful melody over us. I believe that God gave me this picture of Himself to reassure me that He had been with me through all my childhood heartaches; He wanted me to accept Him with a childlike faith. Maybe I was not to work so hard at understanding the complexities but to have freedom to just exist with Him. What an amazing thought, although He may have been communicating something entirely different. I looked to my left at the prayer teams once more and felt as if the idea was not as formidable as I had first believed. Maybe it would be okay to be prayed for tomorrow.

That evening in the service after dinner, I lifted my hands a little and felt such freedom wash over me like never before; I remarked that maybe I had had some sort of vision or dream during prayer that day. I also thought more about celebrating before the Lord in worship and recalled a sermon Paul had given about King David and his wife Michal. The takeaway was this: Scripture tells us that when David entered Jerusalem with the Israelites, who were transporting the Ark from Obed Edom, the whole House of Israel celebrated by leaping and dancing with all their might before the Lord. They rejoiced with songs and harps, lyres, tambourines, and cymbals, and I am sure their hands were raised. Saul's daughter Michal, who was David's wife, looked with disdain upon her husband's revelry, and because of her ridicule in his display of joy, she was barren to the day of her death. Because of that sermon, I had never wanted to be spiritually barren and thought if King David could celebrate and dance before the Lord, then I would not be judged because my hands were lifted a little unto the heavens.

I returned to Connecticut that Sunday evening with a lot on my plate to seriously think about.

Time to Reflect

Supernatural intervention is always disruptive.

1. Can you think of moments when God showed up (whether you knew it was Him or not) and challenged your core belief?
2. If you sensed that it was God, did you embrace it or run from it?

Scripture Study

1. Read 1 Samuel 3:1–11. How did Eli's wisdom help Samuel connect with God?
2. Read Acts 9:1–9. How did God's encounter change Saul?

Chapter 5

Divine Intervention

Unless you people see miraculous signs and wonders, Jesus told him, you will never believe.

—*John. 4:48*

I had never heard the word *prophetic* used in spiritual terms before May 26, 2000. It was a foreign term, at least in this Lutheran's sense of gifts or talents. Paul and I were invited one particular morning to a prayer breakfast in our state capitol in Hartford. I was the vice chair of the Fairfield County committee, and I gratefully look back and thank the guest speaker who had been invited to the breakfast.

After the initial introductions were made from the podium, a distinguished African man rose to give the morning homily. It was Kingsley Fletcher, a Christian tribal king from Ghana. He gave an arousing speech, and in truth, I was captivated from the first few sentences, as I had only seen a few African preachers before, and only on television. However, he said something very disturbing in his final remarks that morning. He shocked everyone by disclosing that he saw great destruction coming and balls of fire falling, with thousands of people perishing. We all sat very quiet as this word was given there in Connecticut. Lord, what in the world was going to happen in Hartford, with thousands perishing? At the time, I did not even think there were thousands who worked in Hartford who could have been hurt from such predicted mass destruction.

I tucked it away and remembered his very sobering words one year and four months later, on September 11, 2001. Yes, great balls of fire had come, and thousands had perished on a day when our world changed forever. However, it did not happen in Connecticut but ninety miles away in Manhattan. I would later come to understand that Fletcher had given this prophetic warning about the World Trade Center as a word of knowledge from God. I wonder if he even recalled his words that warm May morning. I hope I can meet him again one day and ask him.

We introduced ourselves after the event, and during the conversation, Paul and I were invited to a meeting that evening at a large African American church in Hartford. We were drawn to this man's sincerity and strength of authority in his delivery and decided that we should at least make the long trip back from Westport to hear him speak. It was Memorial Day weekend, and facing holiday traffic was not a pleasant thought. We decided to do it. What was there to lose?

Thursday evening's meeting was puzzling, as only fifty people showed up to hear this tribal king of Ghana in a church auditorium that sat at least three thousand. The Northeast really does not have but one or two mega churches, so I was embarrassed for him. I asked myself why people did not support great speakers like this, especially an African giving a speech in an African American mega church. Fletcher walked out onto the stage as stately as he was and pronounced to the handful of us sitting there that he would preach as if there were five thousand in attendance. What a champ. No wonder this guy was a leader of a small nation. I felt relieved (sort of) and a little more relaxed about it all after he said this.

However, the next question from the podium certainly baffled me. He asked those people in the audience who were prophets to stand up. I looked around, thinking no one would stand to such an odd question. Many stood, and I was shocked. To me, a prophet was someone like Moses or Abraham or even Jesus. I had heard those names used as prophets many times in past sermons from Paul, but in the twenty-first century?

Then he made an announcement that there was a woman in the audience who had had an issue of blood for many years. What an incredible thing to say in front of this small crowd. I believe I must have gasped aloud from embarrassment. I had heard that story in the New Testament, but how could he know this situation might have been going on right here? I guess he did, because a woman in the front row stood up, threw her hands in the air, and cried out. He prayed aloud for her in front of the gathering, embarrassing me further, but this time it was about the "issue of blood" and not the number of attendees.

Lord, I thought, *what was Paul getting me into here?* Poor Paul; I was blaming him for most everything these days. After praying for the woman, Fletcher stated there was a second woman among the group who had cried out to the Lord, needing God to change her life; five months earlier, she wanted to take a new road and turn her life around, but she was confused. He also informed the attendees that something had caused this epiphany for her to make this declaration. I sat frozen in my seat and dared not look around. The hair on my neck was prickly.

Wait just a minute, I thought. *Was he addressing my trip to Chicago?*

I mentally counted the months backwards as my mind raced. May, April, March, February, and January. Five months. January was the date that I had decided to turn the other way with God. It was May. Were all forty-nine others in the audience staring at the back of my head? I never raised my hand but could have run out the exit. What else did this Ghanaian leader know?

I later learned that God often gives prophetic words to ordinary people to encourage believers in their walks of faith. That evening, God obviously used Kingsley Fletcher to speak to me. It was the mightiest sermon I'd ever heard by an African preacher. He was definitely the Muhammad

Ali of the religious world. I can still remember where I was sitting: on the edge of my chair, second row from the middle aisle on the end.

He talked about Moses in the book of Deuteronomy, and I could identify with the great leader of the Israelites. Not that I was a prophet, but Moses had been stuck, like me. And that was what I needed to hear. He had circled Mt. Horeb for too long, and God told him it was time to pull up camp and head north. In effect, "stop and change course in life; you've been going in circles for too long."

It was a sermon delivered to hit the mark for both Paul and myself. I certainly did not want to give up and go south. We were looking for some type of reformation in our own lives. I needed a new direction as a dry Lutheran minister's wife, and I wanted to head north. I felt freedom start to course in my veins. That sounds a little corny, but it's true.

During our initial conversation at the Connecticut State House earlier that morning, Fletcher not only invited us to the Thursday evening service but also to have lunch with him on Friday. Again, something seemed to stop us from saying a polite no. I wanted to broach the subject of this prophetic topic he had spoken so authoritatively about. We visited all afternoon and talked about a variety of wonderful subjects concerning God and life. Like a sponge, I did a lot of listening and was fascinated as he shared about his life as a young boy in Ghana; he had an older brother who stuttered and could not be crowned the tribal king, and then he subsequently was educated at Oxford in England. It was one of the most enthralling luncheons I had ever been invited to. At one point, he asked what we needed him to do for us.

We looked at each other quizzically and then said, "Absolutely nothing. We thought we should ask you what we could do for you."

He seemed taken aback. Maybe people were always pressing him for something he could do for them, which was total speculation on my part. We drove him to get a haircut and back to the hotel, where he extended yet another invitation to attend a Hispanic service that evening in Hartford. He said he was their guest speaker and would like us to be his guest. Well, why not? It was a holiday, and we conveniently had no plans. This time, we hung out in the city to avoid traffic. What was God up to? He was up to a lot, as you will read.

Friday, May 28

Over the two days of visits with Kingsley Fletcher, I had listened intently and took in as much information as possible with an open mind. I did not want to miss a thing; I never entertained one judgmental thought about him. Certainly, a tribal king of Ghana could be respected as moral and authentic in his spiritual walk, but I wanted to hear Paul's assessment of our new friend's character. We did attend the packed service that evening, out of curiosity. There were seven hundred people in attendance at the inner-city church Hartford.

Several interesting things happened during the church service. First, it was my initial venture in attending a Hispanic service. When we arrived, the clergy couples were seated across the front row. A very nice cultural custom, I thought. As a Lutheran pastor, Paul was always in the altar area or pulpit, and I sat in the back, on the side, or in the choir loft, but never beside him. That evening, it was nice sitting next to the Rev, as he is affectionately called by many. Maybe I felt I had missed out too many years alone with our children and without Dad next to us. I might have to try this new seating arrangement out.

Second, I watched as all the congregants of the church arrived. Before finding a seat, they came to the chancel area and knelt at the front altar to pray. I sat curiously watching very intense and passionate prayers offered up to God. They seemed to be using their entire bodies as they prayed. Third, during worship, to my utter discomfort and dismay (and judging spirit), a young man got up to dance with a flag. I thought it disrupted the worship and also thought how vain this young man was to want the attention. I should have remembered that even King David danced before the Lord as he brought the Ark of the Covenant into Jerusalem. If I had thought of that on the particular evening, I might not have judged so harshly.

Fourth, to my utter horror, during the preacher's fiery sermon, a rather large man came down the middle aisle, yelling something and taking a seat right at the front pew; he was frothing from the mouth and fell almost at my feet. He said that he was going to "kill Paul." How in the world did he even know the name Paul? I had never laid eyes on this man. Was he speaking about my husband? I immediately wanted out of that front row and would have exited the church if I could have found the door.

Fletcher did not skip a beat and delivered the man of a demoniac spirit (he informed us) in front of our eyes. Wow. I sat glued to the pew. I looked up after keeping my eyes closed, and Paul was on the floor, with his hand on this man's chest (the one who wanted to kill him), while the ushers surrounded them, praying. Fletcher admonished the church by saying, "The doors of the house of the Lord should always be protected with prayer and watchmen." Of course, who could have scripted this scene? Can you even imagine the shock I had in sitting there? I elected to keep my eyes open just in case something else might happen.

Several minutes later, Paul was asked to come to the front of the church, where Fletcher pronounced a prophetic word over him. He tapped his watch three times and said, "Paul Teske, in twenty-one days, the Lord will open three doors for you, and you will be like a kid in a candy store. Any door you choose will be as great as the other two." (You can read more about Paul's miraculous story in his book, *Healing for Today*.)

Fletcher's sermon that Friday evening was titled "The Earthly and Heavenly Fathers' Blessing." It was powerful and extremely emotional for me to sit through. The problem? My earthly fathers had never blessed me in the way he described. After the sermon, I remember feeling totally empty from not having had a dad do that. One thing I did know, however, was that I never had a blessing by the heavenly Father, either.

After the sermon, Fletcher prayed for each of the pastors and their wives on the long front row to the left of us but did not come across the aisle to our side on the right. I had a twinge of disappointment, as I did not want to be passed over by this great man of God.

For goodness sake, we had had lunch with him that afternoon, I thought. *I would have to wait for another day for a touch from God,* I reluctantly told myself.

All was very quiet and calm, and I thought the service was over. Fletcher walked up to the pulpit, took off his beautiful silk jacket, and laid it over his arm, and then he just stood there. I thought he must be as hot as the seven hundred and fifty of us inside the sweltering sanctuary of the simple Hispanic church. Instead of a closing prayer, though, he bowed his head, and in his lovely, British-educated African voice, he announced there was one more person who needed a touch from God. I held my breath in the stillness of the sultry, thick air. Paul gently nudged me in the back.

Me? Did God want me to go up in front of 749 people for whatever Fletcher thought God wanted to do? I felt as if an invisible rope might be pulling me back from walking forward. I did not want to presume he meant me, though.

Finally, when no one stepped forward, I took a deep

breath and decided to take the plunge and go up to stand before this giant man of God. I hesitantly measured each step to the front. I felt as I did the day I gave my life to Jesus as a young girl. Tears were streaming down my face, I remember, as I stood before him. He did not open his eyes, so I thought maybe he did not see me or sense that I was there. Embarrassed, I was about to sneak back to my seat when he suddenly removed his suit jacket from over his arm and gently put it over my head.

I could hear his deep resonant voice through the exquisite fabric. Was it a blessing he was speaking over me? Unfortunately, I cannot remember one word of his prayer. He never touched me, but I fell onto the floor, as if in a frozen heap. I could not move a muscle in either my legs or arms. I could not even move a facial muscle, and there I was on the floor, feeling like a bag of cement. My eyes were closed shut under the jacket. For six long years, I had mocked this sort of thing. In truth, I absolutely had. I had mocked and disbelieved, but whatever this was, it was totally for real. A beautiful aroma permeated the fabric, which smelled like blooming roses and jasmine. The heady fragrance swept over me.

For two hours, Paul said, I wept under that jacket. I wept and wept from the souls of my feet. I heard voices in what sounded like prayers from a foreign nation being spoken over me and also felt as if I might be swimming in an ocean while being healed from a lifetime of junk. I felt so clean and refreshed coming back from wherever I had been on the floor. The jacket was taken away as gently as it had been laid over me. I was led back to my seat, and there beside me in the pew, of all people, was the flag-waver. I apologized to him for my prideful thoughts concerning his behavior earlier that evening during worship and then told him I thought I had been in some kind of deep ocean current. He kindly nodded as if he understood; I wondered later if he had actually been an angel. They probably dance with flags too.

All mayhem had broken out when I hit the floor. Paul said more than four hundred people ran to the altar for prayer. During Fletcher's initial opening remarks of the service, he announced that God had told him there was going to be a mighty outpouring of the Spirit that evening. Little did I know that I would be the first one down for the outpouring to begin. *Oh, ye woman of little faith.* Of course, you must realize after reading this testimonial that I had an earth-shattering paradigm shift over that holiday weekend. How could I now account for this person of the godhead, called the Spirit, while lying smack on the floor without anyone touching me? I repented that night of unbelief and mocking a man who was excited to worship at the altar. I also repented of doubting, like St. Thomas the disciple.

After leaving the service, Paul and I hit Memorial Day traffic, but never in our twenty-three years of marriage had we laughed like we did that evening. We decided that life had become too serious in this business of ministering to people, and we had forgotten how to have fun as a couple. Did it really take a frothing man who crashed a church service, a dancing worshipper, and a candy store prophecy from Kingsley Fletcher to have this much fun driving home?

I know I had become too serious and grumpy with life in general and had not wanted to accept the change in direction that God had shown Paul we were to take. In anticipation of exciting new adventures as Team Teske, we decided to change course and call it our True North as we embarked on this new beginning. We also agreed that starting Sunday, we would sit with one another in the front pew, emulating the Hispanic tradition. We found it was the best thing we ever did and so did our congregation. Recalling the chaplain's initial prayer over Paul at the War College, we decided to wait on God's timing.

After spending the weekend with Fletcher, we hunted for a Christian bookstore in our area and located one in the Catholic church in the next town. We found the only book on their shelf with "Spirit" in the title: *Good Morning, Holy Spirit* by Benny Hinn. We devoured the book in two days. Who was this Holy Spirit, and what did it all mean to us as a couple? After reading it, we decided to attend a conference with three thousand other searching believers in Baltimore. I was there to be a sponge and to be as open-minded as I could.

During a breakout session at the conference, two women who had never met us gave us very specific prophetic words that encouraged our marriage, addressed personal issues, and spoke to our purpose and destiny. For Paul, one of the team members announced that he was not only a marketplace business leader, but a man with pastoral oversight, as an apostle and a builder and leader to take the city. She did not give us the exact city, but I thought it might be for wherever we were going to eventually land in the future.

As for me, they prayed that the treasure chest would once again be opened that I had closed years before. How could they be so accurate with these insights? They did not even know us. Yes, indeed. I had felt unworthy to possess the treasures and gifts God had for me to use. In finishing our prophetic exercise, one woman turned to me and declared (in a rather loud voice) that I was to preach and prophesy, preach and prophesy, preach and prophesy. She proclaimed it three times.

What? I was stunned about this destiny God might be speaking into my life. Good Lord, if she only knew I panicked in front of large groups and could not give a five-minute speech without nausea. Here she had declared for God that I was going to preach and prophesy. My mind was racing, but I held onto every word she was announcing with such authority. In closing our session, one of the women turned to us and declared that when she saw us coming together, she saw us as a "whirling dervish." This dervish connectedness was to defeat the works of the devil when we ministered and stood together in unity in the fight against darkness, and it would be for the very souls of people. It was yet another layer that God was exposing me to and one I had no idea how He was going to play out in my life, but I was curious to see what could possibly be happening next out of a whirling dervish. I would soon find out. Was this all for real? Mixed in the expectancy was a hint of skepticism. Man, I was hardheaded and stubborn.

After these mighty women spoke into our lives, I started praying fervently that a sign from God would confirm the validity of what He wanted me to do. Defeating the devil sounded like a dramatic war scene I would need energy for. How in the world was I going to fight this battle when everything up to this point was out of my conceptual range of understanding? Like the Navy, Paul and I were either going to make it or not. There was just no in between in this call. I was crying out for something that was real and at least made sense. Here is how the conversation went one day after getting the nerve to bring up the subject with God:

"Okay, Lord, I need a sign. Are you for real? Is all this stuff for real? Do you even exist? If you are not for real, I want out of this. I want out of ministry and my marriage. It is too hard, not worth it, and I did not sign up for it. If you are for real, then why don't we use my name Rivers as a sign? No one will ever know. It will just be between you and me."

I also asked three additional questions that I needed answers for: "Do you want me? Do you care for me? And do you really love me?" I never whispered a hint about this to Paul and waited six long, quiet months. I looked everywhere, but never saw my name.

However, several things happened during the six

months. God was ramping up a spiritual season in the church to a higher level. I saw Paul agonize in not seeing change happen as quickly in our congregation, although he used great wisdom and sought the Lord's direction each day. He personally had changed because of his encounter with the Holy Spirit during those six years, while you obviously know how much I struggled. You can understand change as a human being. It can be frightening when the normal routine of life, is interrupted especially in a church setting, where status quo is often comforting. The funny part of this all was that the paradigm shift was nothing so radical. It was simply about healing prayer (okay, prayer is a good thing), anointing the sick with oil (Paul said the Bible tells the elders of the church to incorporate this into their practice), and equipping the saints on prayer teams (everyone can use training and a little more knowledge on how to pray). And therein was the problem. It was simply a trust issue with me and with some in the church, trusting that God and Paul knew what they were doing. As the captain, Paul had to use great wisdom in slowly turning the mother ship in a new direction, with perseverance and gentleness. He had been prepared for this assignment his whole life, but the unease it created was palpable.

I read somewhere that there are only three ways to jump into cold water. One is to take it timidly, step-by-step or an inch at a time; the second is to jump in no holds barred, like the cannon ball approach (which takes guts); the third is to just jump ship before going into the water at all. Those who fully trusted Captain Teske were testing the waters one toe at a time (me), while a few of those hardy souls went for everything they could in the new equation (his entire board), and for some, it was regrettably too hard for comfort (they jumped ship). They left the protective family, and as they did, I quietly resolved to never get too close to anyone to protect my own heart. Obviously, I had abandonment issues that plagued me when good friends left. But God and Paul were best friends, and sometimes, I saw that it was just the two of them walking alone in those early days on the deck of the ship.

Thankfully, both Father God and my husband were especially gentle with me. I had followed Paul all over the world and supported him for a lifetime together, but God was going to be my professor and ready me for more than I had ever bargained for. Thinking back over those years, I had to repent to both of them for not trusting the situation with my soul and my life. I am sure Paul agonized over me most of those years while I was fighting the heavenly shift. I absolutely did not blame him at all. Like all of us in spiritual battles, it was just God and me in the end of this road less traveled. I was out of options, except the one thing I had asked for: the sign.

The Sign

In 2001, a woman in our church offered Paul five thousand dollars to take congregants to a conference in

Toronto she had heard about. It was a weekend that she thought might encourage anyone who attended. It was billed "The Father's Heart Conference." He asked me if I wanted to attend, since I struggled with the issue of father in my own life. Something drew me in on the heart part of the conference title, so I agreed to go.

We loaded the church van with five lay leaders and left for Toronto a day early, due to a blizzard that was forecast for the next day. As we departed Westport, a thick blanket of snow began to fall. So much for the weather forecast. By the time we reached the New York border, heavy blizzard conditions blurred the highway passage and made the road trip that more arduous. We voted to keep going, but about midnight, drained by slow progress, we decided to find food and gas at the next exit.

We made a random right turn and headed down a dark, snow-covered road in search of an open restaurant. After driving several miles with no luck in the small town, we decided to head the other direction. As we made the U-turn, I looked out of the icy window and saw a little wooden shack on the side of the road that was closed for the night. The sign on the roof read "Angel's Restaurant, Fried Chicken." Fried chicken happened to be my favorite food growing up in Texas; I could probably eat two, if I tried. The bold, black sign was somewhat strange for an eating establishment, I thought. Maybe divine? Angel's Restaurant?

However, what caught my eye in the seventeen-inch snowstorm was the large, white sign with yellow blinking lights illuminating the falling snow on the front yard of the little wooden shack. There were two words on that sign that stunned me. The sign read "Rivers Wanted." I could not believe my eyes. I looked again as the van slowly made its way down the snow-laden road. I had asked God for a sign to validate His existence and requested He use just my name so I'd know it was from Him.

I think I was always waiting to hear my name somewhere but never expected to see it on an actual sign. For whatever reason, it was just a flat-out miracle. God had given me a real, honest- to- goodness sign using my name, just as I had proposed. But He also said something as profound as using my first name on that white blinking board. He said "Wanted." He wanted me. Remember the three questions I asked? I had asked God if He loved me and if He even wanted me. That is how God started to weave Himself into me, like a giant quilt. It would dawn on me later that weekend that I had never thought about my own name, *Rivers*, in the word *Drivers*. I guess the "D" had fallen off the sign in the snow, which was meant to read, "Drivers Wanted." Really.

I was stunned. Whatever had happened to that letter "D" didn't matter; however, the sign, which read "Rivers Wanted," did matter. It was a game-changer. My life was now turned upside down. Have you ever thought about how funny God is? He has such a hilarious sense of humor when He pops into a life for good. Actually, He is a genius. This one massive, miraculous act of God (an actual sign) changed my life forever that evening in upstate New York, and it has never been the same since. My reformation of soul and spirit could not have been more divinely planned than that.

After twenty or so grueling hours on the road, we arrived at the Toronto church to attend the Father's Heart Conference. It was a two-day conference with various speakers and topics geared to issues of family, crisis management, and the Father's love. We could all identify with the subject matter. There was a soaking prayer room I found on the agenda that piqued my interest. One could just lie on a pillow and meditate quietly to the beautiful strains of a harp or violin being played. I found this room to be extremely soothing and calming to my emotional and physical state, albeit uniquely different. I could do nothing but worship God on my back with my eyes closed and lose myself in the fact that He had wanted me, as the sign had read.

I hope you can understand the depth of what this did to my heart and my life after so many years of doubt, worry, unease, and fear. He absolutely saved me and wants to save you.

The Father Wound

Later in the evening, Jack Winter, a visiting pastor, asked for pastors and their wives to come forward if they would like prayer. In all the years of ministry we had participated in, no one had ever prayed for us as a couple, which is an absolute travesty. Not since our wedding ceremony twenty-three years earlier had we been blessed as one, in the Lord. We must have bounded down the aisle from the back of the auditorium in sheer desperation to meet Pastor Winter, as we were the first in line to ask for that special covering prayer. His attention was directed toward Paul first, and he asked what type of relationship he had had with his earthly father. "Great, he was an awesome dad," was his reply. I concurred wholeheartedly that Mr. Teske was an awesome dad.

When he turned to and asked me the same question, I began weeping uncontrollably. Paul answered for me while I gathered my composure. Winter reminded me of a grandfatherly type, with a barrel chest and such kind eyes. He said he was going to give me an earthly father's blessing by standing in for my two fathers. I am pretty sure four thousand people must have heard the wails from the pit of my stomach as he prayed over me. Honestly, this was not the reaction I thought I could ever exhibit during a prayer before a crowd, but it concerned my fathers, and my broken heart needed healing from these relationships.

When and where was the Orthodox blessing of the father lost on our human family? Why didn't the Protestants and Catholics cherish this tradition and rite of passage over their families? It was certainly lost on mine. We have found the Father's Blessing to be the single most critical act of love a father can do for his sons and daughters. I would first have to forgive my two fathers in order to be released, and that was a difficult step to finalize in front of Pastor Winter. And therein lies the problem of why people view God the way they do. The earthly father is the conduit or the lens through which we see the heavenly Father. These were deeply walled issues of my own heart that ultimately had to be addressed and healed: physical and emotional abandonment, mistrust, feeling unwanted and unloved, and, at the core, shame.

Hence the request for the sign I needed from God. Was I wanted? Your list may differ. It might include abuse, absenteeism, control, violence, bullying, even early death. I want to emphasize that we all have issues, because we are human, and humans fail. But if your relationship with your father has been wonderful, then I celebrate that. However, you may have a friend who has not had that closeness and missed a large chunk of unconditional love.

That night, the most poignant touch was going to be from the heavenly Father, which Pastor Winter administered a few minutes later. It was the trust part in my personal relationship with God that I needed to heal in order to reconcile with Him. Could I trust God? That was the most loaded question to work through in the prayer time. I figured all the conference participants must have needed help with father issues that evening; about two thousand people poured into the aisles as I left the stage area. I was not going to be alone in this quest for the holes in a heart that needed to be stitched up. I do not think I could have had the heartache healed and the trust restored with the father's love that night had I not first seen "Rivers Wanted" on the restaurant sign. Thank You, Jesus, right?

The final piece in this quilt of God was being sewn into place by His very own hands, and the piece was labeled "Divine Love." This love is almost incomprehensible to people. Ultimately, this is what we all have in common as the created race: to be loved and to be wanted in life. It gave a weighty heaviness of reassurance that God the Father accepted me unconditionally. The assurance also gave me a total peace knowing that within the safety net, I could trust God to help me forge ahead in this crazy new spiritual life, walking beside my husband. I was in uncharted territory, but it was all I needed to run with.

Yes, Pastor Winter stood in for my fathers so I could forgive them, and then he blessed me as a daughter of King God. The hardest journey was ahead for me, as I learned to apply the trust that had been addressed. I would have to trust that God knew exactly what He was doing in my life, my marriage, and my spiritual journey. He was a good God and would carry me along even in the rougher waters when they were to come in life. I was His, and I could trust He wanted only the very best for me.

In closing this chapter out, the sign "Rivers Wanted" was the beginning of the most beautiful and humbling journey, with the loving Father and my husband by my side.

Prayer

Father God, we know your ways are not always our ways, but your ways are, without a doubt, the only way. Help us release our agendas to pursue life, and allow us by your Holy Spirit to surrender to your pathway. We are confident that you will never lead us astray and that you only have what is best for us, which is our destiny. Father, I know that you love these people unconditionally and that you will never abandon or leave them. We are wanted by you, Lord God, now and forever. Help us, Lord, not to look back and have any regrets. In Jesus's name, Amen.

Time to Reflect

1. Have you ever asked God for a sign to speak to your heart to confirm a specific question?
2. Have you ever thought of yourself as a throwaway or unwanted by people or God or both?

Scripture Study

1. Read Isaiah 7:11 and Isaiah 38:7. Is it okay to ask the Lord for a sign?
2. Read Judges 6. Does this narrative about Gideon give you hope when seeking the Lord's guidance?

Chapter 6

Women at the Well

Deep calls to deep in the roar of your waterfalls;
all your waves and breakers have swept over me.

—Psalm 42:7

Shortly after returning from Toronto, it dawned on me one day that people were more afraid of God the Holy Spirit than they were of the devil. I could understand this, as I had juggled with the same doubts and fears. I want to say upfront, do not waste your time in trying to figure out all that the Spirit does. I regret all the lost years I tried to do it. He is the powerhouse within us and is there to comfort, encourage, and give counsel. It is a deep mystery known only to God how He touches our lives and empowers us when we need it the most. While the mind can be a battleground and full of curiosity, it is not about trying to figure it out. It simply unfolds as a mystery in a person's life when the Spirit is breaking into the unfamiliar.

At least that is what happened as I grew deeper and stronger with the Lord. I do not know where I would be today had God not interrupted my life (more like invaded) in such dramatic ways, but I was not going to be the ultimate event planner; He was. However, I did resolve shortly after Toronto that if Jesus needed the Spirit in the valley of temptation, then the Spirit was going to be good enough for me. Either we choose to come out of our desert seasons in a daze, to wonder what happened in the losing battle, or we choose to come out powerfully, refreshed, wiser, and certainly more alert for the next onslaught when it occurs. Get ready, though; it will occur if one is doing the work of God.

March 17, 2002, was a beautiful Sunday morning at church; the congregation was about to be introduced to the Holy Spirit. Just so you know, God will always start in His house at the top when a mighty shift is coming. The head of the church is God's authority in action. As Paul has taught, "As the head goes, so goes the body." In his wisdom, he also taught me to believe that if God can entrust us with the small things, He can entrust us with the more powerful plans He is going to accomplish in the body of believers. I was not fully prepared, but I was willing. I do not believe anyone in our congregation had ever witnessed a person being gently overwhelmed with the Spirit like that morning, but I found myself curiously on the floor, alongside my husband.

Harald Bredesen, our dear elderly pastor-at-large, had visited St. Paul's Westport the previous week and had given us a blessing and powerful words of encouragement on the front row, which honored us as the leaders before the church. I had never been called "good and faithful servant" until this particular Sunday, so my heart was soaring and truly blessed by his powerful words. We were taken by surprise by a young woman who had invited us to stand together as a couple in front of the altar after dear Harald's visit. She laid her hands on our shoulders and started praying. In my prayer journal, I wrote that the music was beautiful and soft that morning when we were prayed over. I remembered the words of the prophetic team in Baltimore given to Paul: "do not hold back," and leaned over to whisper them into his ear as we stood together. I have no idea why I did that, it just came out. My right arm was lightly interlocked with Paul's left arm, and I felt my knees buckle and fell backwards onto the floor, with him by my side. The most amazing thing was that it felt like a gentle and slow fall, almost like feathers drifting to the floor. There was no one behind us to catch our fall.

I am sure the congregation was shocked to see their Lutheran pastor and his wife on the floor that day. I never knew whether we had any visitors that day and imagine they might have run out the front door. However, while on the floor, I felt a heavy presence come over me like a thick cloud; I could not move one muscle. Believe me, I was trying.

I was taken to a distant, quiet place somewhere

in the universe and remember it felt so holy there. Instantaneously, I felt a welling sensation bubble up from deep within my body, almost as if a deep cry from my belly. Actually, I recall telling God in my mind, *Please do not let the people be afraid of whatever this is.* I double-checked my dream journal for the exact words. The voice (not my own) cried out, "I am the Lord your God; where are my people? I love them so very much; where are my people? I love them so very much. I want your hearts. I am sad and brokenhearted. I want to be with my people."

I was then taken to an ancient well. What I believe is this: God was calling out to the global church from His Spirit and not just for our congregation in Westport. He just happened to address His longing for the universal church while I was on the floor of our Lutheran church in Connecticut. I prayed that we could handle all of this.

It is still amazing to think that the voice of God spoke through me like this. Who was I? Perhaps even more astonishing to the whole event was the actual trip to the well in the hot, arid desert of the ancient times. I knew I was there as a participant to observe the lives of women and children of those times. However, I was not frightened to be there, as it seemed perfectly fine and normal to watch the scene unfold before me. How fascinating to see the biblical days come alive. The Spirit seemed to impress on me that He was showing me how women ministered to one another, since they were not allowed into the temple, and also how they performed daily responsibilities of family life at the all-important community well.

This may seem like a trivial comparison, but in order to describe the experience of simply being transported to a place in ancient times, it might help for readers to recall Charles Dickens's *A Christmas Carol*. This is the only thing that comes to mind if you will allow me. If you will remember, first the audience is introduced to the old miser, Ebenezer Scrooge, who hates Christmas. His treatment of fellow employee Bob Cratchit on the eve of Christmas sets up the infamous visit of the ghost of Christmas past, as he is led back in time to observe his growing love of money and abhorrent treatment of people. He had lessons to learn from his past in order for him to make the ultimate declaration, yes, that he wanted to live and be a better person. As the audience, we are brilliantly brought into each moment with Scrooge to capture the essence of community life with scenes full of characters, festivities, foods, celebrations, and the emotions of daily English life. My experience in the desert was much like this as I observed the scenes at the well (of course, not taken by the hand of any ghost of Old Testament past).

Have you ever wondered what a woman's life was like in the Old Testament? First, the throngs of women and children coming to socialize amazed me as I watched. The well was central to their way of living in the desert. The children ate and played with friends while older women sat down to chat after drawing water for their homes and livestock. How amazing that I was able to take in every detail of the scene such as colors, sounds, activities, and the clothing being worn. Much like the biblical days, today's modern woman entertains these same aspects of communal living. As a former apparel designer, I was intrigued by the fashions of the Old Testament women. The colors of the tunics, belts, and headdresses were a mixture of brilliant hues of purples, blues, reds, and golden yellows, while earth tones were juxtaposed like the desert sands. I listened as the young women harmonized beautiful songs while the small groups of women gathered around the well. They were singing. Another group of women were making small cakes. They shook large, tightly woven baskets of grain and hummed these musical tunes. It was all in rhythm, while yet another group washed clothes and bathed the babies from the small reservoir close by. The heat was staggering in the desert, but I saw older women sitting under a small bush, the only shade tree I could see, while teaching younger women the simple lessons of the Jewish faith, family responsibility, and stories handed down about the bravery of the Israelites.

I somehow felt in the Spirit that this was where the young women and children were learning lessons from the Torah as their brothers and cousins were being taught in a synagogue or a tent in the village. I was contented to know that the young women were not spiritually left behind and that the grandmothers and mothers cared for one another so beautifully and respectfully, as they ministered concerning the God of Abraham, Isaac, and

Jacob. I imagined that the grandmothers had to reprimand any siblings or friends who had petty issues. After the vision, I returned to scripture that week to study Rachel and Leah and learn how they might have chosen sides with other women in their dislike or jealousy over their husbands. The well was a place for not only water but for the culture of everyday life.

In comparison to our modern-day world, we, too, have wells of healing and ministry as women of God, just as our ancient sisters experienced. Our wells are the kitchen tables, luncheons, mother's groups, visiting the sick, teaching a class, presenting a paper, taking a road trip, attending a conference, driving a child to school, sharing with a shop owner who cares, going on mercy missions, and more. Where there is a woman, there is a well.

The vision ended, and I slowly opened my eyes to see several women congregants of St. Paul's peering over me while I was flat on my back. I giggled (I think) and told them I hoped no one had been afraid of what had happened. I also was hoping they knew me well enough to know that I'd never choose to do such a thing on my own. Almost fifty people from the church jumped ship that day. It was just too much for them to handle in our little Antioch-like island of safety. For the ones who stayed, they were in for the ride of their lives. Just like the Acts church of the New Testament, the journey would include a fork in the road, where people were going to have to choose between going for God or traditional complacency.

Time to Reflect

1. Do you have anyone in your life with whom you can share your most intimate and personal experiences without feeling judged?
2. Knowing that God has an intimate knowledge of your life, do you believe in your heart that He loves you without condemnation?

Scripture Study

1. Read John 4:1–30. Have you ever had an encounter with Jesus like the Samaritan woman at the well?
2. Read John 4:28. Have you set your bucket (life's priorities) down to pursue Jesus as your number one priority in life?

Chapter 7

A Lion's Heart, the Church, and the Rider

The Lord your God is with you, the Mighty Warrior who saves. He will take great delight in you; in his love he will no longer rebuke you but will rejoice over you with singing.

—Zephaniah 3:17

One beautiful June morning in the Upper Room at our church in Westport, I had three succinct visions. It also happened to be our twenty-third wedding anniversary. A small prayer group of four met as usual to pray for the needs of our congregation. I had come to love this time we spent together in lifting up our families and pressing issues we were tasked with. Lately, we had gone deeper in our prayer and always agreed afterwards that we had felt such intimacy and connection with God during these weekly sessions. On this particular day, Kevin Mardorf, who was a dedicated member of our prayer team, asked for prayer because he was recently diagnosed with heart disease. He was a forty-year-old leader in our church and a great young man of God, whom Paul considered a spiritual flank. I considered him to have the heart of a lion. He was strong, courageous, and such a ferocious fighter for the Kingdom and anything pertaining to what God needed us to battle for. I am reminded of this verse for him:

The Lion's Heart

> *Then even the bravest soldier, whose heart is like the heart of a lion, will melt with fear, for all Israel knows that your father is a fighter and those with him are brave.*

(2 Samuel 17:10)

I loved Kevin's pastoral encouragement for my husband and the loyal support he and his family always gave to ours. As our prayer intensified in the circle that morning, I surprisingly found myself standing in a serene and holy place outside of the prayer room, actually feeling the beating of Kevin's heart in my own. It was the strangest sensation and something I had, of course, never experienced before. I could hear the pounding thumps against my chest, which sounded so strong as if mine were in sync with his. I could hear our prayer group in the near vicinity ask God for a complete healing of the aorta and the damaged muscles. During this vision, I also saw his heart being wrapped in white, over and over again, as if it was a beautiful cocoon. It was a lovely, protective white linen material. I was fascinated that Jesus was allowing me to see his heart being totally healed in such a supernatural way and wrote down later in my journal that I was having this whole conversation with God while still in the vision.

After this vision ended, I was immediately taken into the second one, observing our church united in a glorious worship service. Our sanctuary has forty-foot vaulted wooden ceilings and a lovely acoustical reverberation. The sanctuary was packed that day, and each congregant was beautifully dressed in white as the resplendent music soared to the ceiling rafters. Every glorious voice seemed to be lifted up in great strength and harmony. The roof was opened to the heavens (much like a modern-day domed football stadium), and I saw the church building sitting in the palm of God's massive hands. His enormous face beamed down over the worship team on the right side of the church sanctuary as He listened to us sing. His kind face was framed by snow-white hair. I peered out the long glass window. Standing on the sidewalk outside of our brick church were three people I knew from our congregation, a couple from South Africa and a new member. God's blazing red eyes shot like lasers through their bodies at an angle. It was shocking that the bright ray of red beams streamed right through their bodies from God's eyes onto the sidewalk. What was God seeing?

As I was contemplating this question, I was immediately taken into a third vision to the front of the church grounds, which has a wide circular drive off of the main road.

The Rider on the White Horse

I saw heaven standing open and there before me was a white horse, whose rider is called Faithful and True. With justice he judges and wages war. His eyes are like blazing fire, and on his head are many crowns. He has a name written on him that no one knows but he himself.

(Revelation 19:11–12)

From both busy street entrances, the church and entire property was covered in sparkling gold, like rain particles falling from the sky. Even cars driving in front of our large building were blasted with a dense gold going through the seventy-yard stretch from entrance to exit. Into the golden wall of rain and out the other side they drove. I could hear the perplexed drivers exclaiming, "What in the world just hit me?" I surmised it must be the glory of God hitting them and happily hoped the glory would stick to encourage them in every issue of their life. Surrounding the ten-acre perimeter of the church property, I turned to see a twenty-foot boxwood hedge so dense and so incredibly tightly woven, a hand could not penetrate through the tiny branches. Standing on the interior side of the hedge and facing the church were thousands of magnificent silver shields that touched point to point. These costly armored protectors of war were approximately fifteen feet in height and shimmered, as if alive. It was an astonishing scene of security and beauty that I felt as we were hemmed in this safe haven with Jesus. These could have been the literal shields of faith and the hedges of protection written about in this passage of Ephesians below:

> Finally, be strong in the Lord and in his mighty power. Put on the full armor of God, so that you can take your stand against the devil's schemes. For our struggle is not against flesh and blood, but against the rulers, against the authorities, against the powers of this dark world and against the spiritual forces of evil in the heavenly realms. Therefore put on the full armor of God, so that when the day of evil comes, you may be able to stand your ground, and after you have done everything, to stand. Stand firm then, with the belt of truth buckled around your waist, with the breastplate of righteousness in place, and with your feet fitted with the readiness that comes from the gospel of peace. In addition to all this, take up the shield of faith, with which you can

> *extinguish all the flaming arrows of the evil one.*
> *Take the helmet of salvation and the sword of the*
> *Spirit, which is the word of God. And pray in the*
> *Spirit on all occasions with all kinds of prayers*
> *and requests. With this in mind, be alert and*
> *always keep on praying for all the Lord's people.*
>
> *(Ephesians 6:10–18)*

My attention was then drawn to a victorious Jesus, Who appeared on His personal stallion in front of our church along the driveway, inside the shimmering and dense barriers of protection. It was the healthiest and most magnificent white horse I had ever seen. He was like the stallion in the movie *War Horse*. He stood approximately twenty-four hands high; his pure white tail and mane were long and flowing. His coat looked as if it had been brushed to a glossy sheen. This was the mightiest beast I had ever seen in the animal kingdom. He carried the Savior of the world, and I was awestruck. Of course, there could be nothing but perfection to carry the King.

Jesus sat atop the horse without a saddle and was dressed in those crisp white linen robes that I was becoming so familiar with. His back was straight like a champion, while His beautiful wavy brown hair fell softly to broad shoulders. Definitely the gallant King was here to pronounce something over us all. In His right hand, He was carrying a tall golden pole, which was anchored on His right thigh. On the pole was an exquisite white satin banner, whose edges were trimmed in an array of white fringe, gently blowing in the slight breeze. The horizontal red crimson letters on the banner spelled "LOVE." I was moved by the awesome declaration of our Mighty King Jesus. Behind the triumphant rider and horse were thousands upon thousands of saints singing, dancing, and celebrating with tambourines in the driveway. It was not only our church congregation but saints of the global church.

This grand event reminded me of the scripture that addresses the banner of love: "Let him lead me to the banquet hall and let his banner over me be love" (Song of Songs 2:4). Maybe the throngs I had seen celebrating behind the victorious Jesus were on their way to the banqueting table. We were going to celebrate with the King, who was honored and glorified by the crowds.

The vision lifted, and I was immediately brought back into the circle for closing prayer time, to which I was only able to say a quiet, "Amen." These visions were beginning to rock my personal world. Why had God just allowed me to see the beauty of the Lord and His banner over us, which was love? Were the hedges for protection from the outside world? Was the golden rain His glory? What did it all mean?

The next morning, the worship team taught us a new piece we had heard several weeks before. The worship piece was titled *His Banner over Us Is Love, Love, Love.* How could the worship leader have known what I was about to share in church from the Upper Room experience the day before? What a genius God we have. His messaging is always on target and on time, especially in matters of the heart. Yes. He is our strength and our salvation, and His banner of love flows eternally over us. We will praise the Lord forever. Selah.

Sadly, Kevin Mardorf passed away soon after our prayer session from a sudden heart attack. To a deeply grieving pastor and church body, we laid him to rest, but I personally knew deep within my own heart that the Lord had shown me his entire heart being supernaturally healed in the Upper Room, wrapped in eternal white linen in heaven, signifying purity. I was utterly amazed by these three visions and had so many questions for God.

Time to Reflect

1. How does this cascade of visions speak to your heart?
2. Do you find them encouraging and uplifting? If so, how?

Scripture Study

1. Read Revelation 1:9–11. When you read this chapter, did the voice of God speak to you in anyway? If so, how?
2. Read Revelation 19:11–12. Knowing that the battle belongs to God, can you trust Jesus with all your victories?

Chapter 8

The Followers of Jesus

I, a poor, miserable sinner, confess unto thee.

—*The Lutheran Confessional*

Late one afternoon, Paul called from church and excitedly asked if I would like to go to Rome in two days. That was considered spur of the moment, even for him, but he had secured discounted tickets; I made several mental calculations and decided I could pull it off. He made arrangements to have a travel agent book a hotel room while we were in flight, and off we went to discover Italy. I was always thrilled to pack bags and go to exotic places. Really, when is it that a husband can find great tickets and call up to say, "Let's go"?

Arriving in Rome was crazy. The airport was jammed with hustling international visitors; the Italian airport personnel were vivacious, somewhat accommodating, and totally, well, Italian. The love for life for Italians is bigger than Texas, as one would say. After waiting for hours in baggage claim, our luggage was unfortunately announced lost. It was explained away simply as, *"Se la vie; it is just life."* It was not exactly how we wanted to start our great trip, but I guess we could deal, if the Italians thought we could. After a harrowing ride by taxi, the travel agent in Los Angeles was golden, as we found our small hotel off of a quiet Roman street by the Spanish Steps he had procured for us. Our luggage would not arrive for three days, but it was the best plan that God had for us. This was Rome, and we were on an adventure with each other, so nothing was going to rain on our parade. The slip-on leather-soled shoes would have to suffice on the old bricks, although it was tricky maneuvering the tourist sites and walking tours. Se la vie; I could be tough. It was my electric hair curlers that I could not live without, here on earth or in heaven; I had hand-carried them in my purse. The ladies will understand. Later that night, the electric transformer I carried for the rollers blew up. Oh well. Wild hair and one wrinkly black New York outfit pretty much summed up what I looked like on my exotic Roman holiday. However, my senses soared as we took in every detail of the ancient city and its architectural gems from the taxi that whizzed through the streets. I soon forgot what I was going to look like in all the photos. The creative genius of the historical artisans and the truckloads of magnificent Italian marble they used on every edifice that could be built has captivated art lovers for centuries, including myself.

Rome certainly could be a heady experience when visiting for the first time. I don't want to overly dramatize (too late?), but the reoccurring thoughts I had during the week was how these ancient artisans had been used by God to beautify the church structures and city buildings with the majesty of imagination and architectural prowess. How did they paint upside down? What did they feel when they were celebrated for their fresco masterpieces engulfing the vaulted ceilings? Where had they received the detailed blueprints of beauty: at a table, in a dream, over Italian coffee with God? Who were their friends? Did they paint alone? Were they afraid to fall from the wooden scaffolding lifted, oh so high? How did they maintain their eyesight and health while they painted in dim candlelight? And what about their vision when finished; could they continue to take on new tedious projects?

My mind was racing with all these thoughts as I rediscovered the artistic side of myself that was absolutely famished and dry for exploration, art, romance, and ancient history. I had missed my music, which I had buried in a hole so long ago. I tried to breathe in the air of this artist colony, to feel it to the core of my soul. I never had the opportunity to experience or explore an ancient city while growing up in Texas. My life was about weekends at the grandparents' farm, learning to fish, riding to town in the back of a truck, finding armadillo hideouts, shooting a pistol, or tearing up the hay barn for imaginary houses. It was not about mosaic floors, Venetian chandeliers,

Roman columns, or miniature corner cathedrals passing for extravagant mini Vaticans on cobblestone streets. My life as a child was also not about exquisite inlaid woods, ancient Roman ruins, or Italian marbles. I sighed to think of technology invading our nondescript lives in modern times. What an absolute privilege to grow up in the ancient cities of Europe and to experience all of this. I hope young Europeans appreciate all the culture they have to live with on a daily basis. At dusk each evening in Rome, we were greeted by a single violin's melodious notes as we rounded the small, winding stone streets heading for our quaint hotel. Beautiful music has a magical way of lifting a tired soul, hurting feet, and hungry stomachs. Where was this musician? Was he or she on a roof or hanging out of an Italian window somewhere below? We fell in love all over again in this great Roman town. It was on the third day that Paul suggested we visit Rome's large cathedral, the Basilica of St. John Lateran, where the seat of Christendom for the Catholic Church resided. Kings had been crowned in this church, he told me, and popes had been commissioned at the massive marble altar. It was the city's first church, and the adjoining Lateran Palace was the home to the popes until they left for Avignon, France, in 1305. He thought I would enjoy the historical value of this particular tourist site. We ran across the street in the pouring rain, dodging puddles and taxis to get into the ancient basilica. I will never forget the moment we walked through the intricately carved double doors. The wood was about twelve inches thick and so heavy, a special staff associate was present to close them. Stepping into the narthex, I became very emotional and started to cry. Several visitors stared at me (probably assuming I was suffering from jet lag).

An electrical current shot through my body as we walked through the simple, stark white portico into the grand sanctuary awaiting us. I was perplexed and surprised by this unexpected outburst. I mean, I was just there to see a cathedral that Paul thought might be interesting. What was going on with me? I seemed to feel okay. We walked into the grand hall, and there, in the vaulted room, stood replicas of the twelve martyred apostles of Jesus, including Apostle Paul. I remembered this reference in Matthew 10:1: "Jesus called his twelve disciples to him and gave them authority to drive out impure spirits and to heal every disease and sickness."

I felt an incredible energy swirling around me, as if it were just these incredible marble giants communing together with me as they lined the outer aisles of the imposing basilica. Each carved replica depicted how the martyr had died for Christ. My heart was torn for them. What suffering must they have endured in their last hours on earth? Was this why I had sensed a hidden emotional sadness coming through the front door? I was struck by the facial features of the chiseled stroke of the sculptor on each marbled statue. I fell onto a kneeler in front of the Cross and suddenly felt like a paltry flea. What had I done for Jesus? *Not much*, I thought. *Nada. Nothing.* I sat devastated as the truth hit me. I silently wept for the world and for myself that day. I felt as if I had come to a crossroad in my own life, which seemed to have halted at this very tourist spot. The crazy business of programs, kids' sports, schools, job, and church flashed before my eyes. What was so important in my life that I had never given enough thought to these courageous apostles before this trip? Did the sculptor know the effect his works of art would have on travelers like myself? If Paul had not been with me, I could have curled up on the small wooden bench for the night to be in this holy place with the humble saints of ages past. Up to this point, I had been a loyal wife; I prayed that my children thought of me as a good mother. I was a chaplain's wife, a minister's wife, a committee member, a passionate American, but what I was not was a sold-out follower of Jesus. Was I an utter failure in my mission for Christ? *Probably*, the accusing voice in my head confirmed. The remorse I felt for the wasted years left me empty and void. These valiant, beautiful, mighty men of God were inspired by Him personally and stayed the course for Christendom at their appointed time in history. God loved them and knew they would be the world changers before the beginning of time. They were the chosen ones to perform miracles, signs, and wonders in the power of the Spirit. What had been their suffering end? They had all died horrific, martyred deaths, believing in their leader, their friend, their Savior, this Jesus. These simple heroic men were fishermen, a physician, a Greek philosopher, a Roman citizen, and a terrorist to Christians; all had at the allotted time been totally sold out to God's salvation plan through Jesus. They had been chosen by God and said yes to take the Gospel out to the ends of the dying world, which unbelievably still flourishes today. I was so proud of them.

The incalculable personal cost of this courageous and dedicated journey of spreading the good news was a death sentence for each apostle. For those they touched; one just had to believe, one just had to have simple faith that Jesus loved the world and died on a Cross for it; one just had to believe that God's Son died for their sin and was Resurrected to live forever. They had been beheaded, beaten, skinned alive, stoned to death, boiled in hot oil, and crucified upside down on a cross. These were all lovers and followers of Jesus. These great heroes stared at me in St. John the Lateran, their lives (and deaths) beckoning me on to a personal and higher level in ministry and service for the Lord.

What must the sculptor have felt as he carved these brave souls out of massive blocks of marble? Did God Himself choose each piece of marble for the honorable band of brothers? I believe He loved them so much that He actually did this small act of creative kindness, pointing the way to the marble yard for the artist. We heard a wonderful story on our tour of Florence about the Renaissance artist, Michelangelo. He had carved the famous *David* out of a block of marble that had sat in his patron's courtyard for over twenty-five years before chosen to be his famous masterpiece. It is said that he claimed that his job was to "free the human form that had been trapped inside the block of stone." I can see why he would have known this after my own visit to see the breathtaking statue of the great young shepherd of the Bible. Of course, God had divinely saved that piece for the young artist's sculptor's tool. How could it have been any other way?

The monumental pioneers of the early church who stood before me were something else. They stood for bravery, courage, pioneering, strength, faithfulness, martyrdom, love, passion, and brotherhood. What must the artist have felt about God as he created these forms of the beloved followers carved into the stucco alcoves? Had any of the thousands of worshippers in these same wooden pews felt as I about these worthy giants? I had so many unanswered questions. The tears flowed as I turned my life over to the cause of Christ at the simple but stately altar. Thank You, God, for this incredible encounter, and thank You that our luggage was lost on our first Roman holiday.

I left St. John's the Lateran that late day, determined to find the scope of what I was as a woman in Jesus. It would take a few more crooked roads of my personal journey to straighten out, but the Spirit was setting up a perfect storm for my life. I was on a quest, if anything, to find it and needed to hear from God Himself. I was hungry and thirsty for God. Scripture says, "'The days are coming,' declares the Sovereign Lord, 'when I will send a famine through the land—not a famine of food or a thirst for water, but a famine of hearing the words of the Lord'" (Amos 8:11).

Several months later, a call went out for Sunday school teachers at church. The committee was short a few adults to handle classes. My hand shot up, although I had never taught a class. I figured I would be safe if I volunteered for discussions in the sweet five-year-old classes. I would not have to be the perfect Bible professor like my husband; however, I wanted the stories to come alive for the little ones, like the giants had come alive for me on the trip to Rome. Of course, God had other plans because it was not really going to be about the children but about my relationship with Him. He was going to be my teacher and sole professor for a lifetime. I was awakened at three o'clock each morning, and that is how it all really started. It was the most incredible time to have intimate communication with the Master. It was while writing this chapter on the followers of Jesus that I had a crazy epiphany: God was actually painting His own piece of artwork for the new chapter in my life by giving me incredible visions and dreams on our educational journey of the Spirit, which is the genesis (no pun intended) for this book you are reading. What a genius He is.

I became an avid, insatiable student at the Master's feet for two years and twenty-nine days every morning at the appointed time of three o'clock. After studying scripture, I would lie in front of the fireplace face down, turn on Terry McAlmon worship music, and listen for hours. I was almost ready to step out.

Time to Reflect

1. Have you ever thought about the martyred death of the apostles?
2. Up to this point in your life, what great price have you paid for Jesus?

Scripture Study

1. Read John 15:13. How does this passage speak to your heart?
2. Read Philippians 1:20–24. Reflect on your personal view of life and death in relationship to being with Jesus Christ.

Chapter 9

The Fifth Seal

*Then the Lord replied: "Write down the
revelation and make it plain on tablets so that a
herald may run with it. For the revelation awaits
an appointed time; it speaks of the end and will
not prove false. Though it linger, wait for it; it
will certainly come and will not delay."*

—*Habakkuk 2:2–3*

Desert beauty has always fascinated me from a
distance. I have never lived near a desert, but I have seen
several in the world where sustainability looks impossible,
until you take a closer look at the thriving ecosystems.
I have seen the vast desert regions in Israel, the white
desert sand dunes and safari of the Namibian coastlines,
the Middle Eastern Sahara, and arid areas of Africa and
Australia. How do people survive in such extreme heat
and dust? How hard is it to plant food to subsist on or find

water to exist or find fuel for machinery? It all seems so difficult to live and thrive in these desert spaces.

I also know from my own life and hearing stories of others that the deserts of people's lives can be compared to those sandy regions. Life can be dry, dusty, empty, lonely, and sometimes hopeless, until the true well of life, Jesus, fills the deepest void with living water. Have you ever felt like you've been wandering around for forty years, like the Israelites did, with a dry heart or soul? Was it the same for the early wanderers in scripture? I confess it could have been much easier for me personally in walking the dust trails, if I had not been so prideful and too stubborn to the call of God on my life. I was too busy trying to sort it out in my own strength. Just like the Israelites, I was completely rebellious; when I think of it, it is an improbable miracle we even survive ourselves as a collective people.

There are few words to convey my gratitude that God had the ultimate plan for my life's purpose and stuck with me. I know, with God, there is only possibility for a positive result in sticking with His purpose and plan. There will be ultimate success in the end only with Him. I certainly could not see beyond the grief and pain before the vision of heaven, but He did. I could not see beyond the phobia and fears of darkness and dying, but He did. I could not see beyond the pain of a family heartache, but He did. I have come to understand this: that the Holy Spirit waits patiently, nudges gently, and then makes His move at just the right time. It is said around our house that God is never late, He is never early, and He is always on time. In truth, I would not have had the patience with myself, but then, I am not God. If you are not familiar with some of the names He is called in the Bible, two of His mighty names are Long Suffering and Patience, and for that, I am most grateful.

On a recent trip to New York, we were able to see a special exhibition of the Dead Sea Scrolls and read about the tremendous treasure trove of discovery for the twentieth- and twenty-first-century historical findings. Of course, having visited the Dead Sea myself, I knew the vast stretch of desert, which led to the caves where the scrolls were discovered. It was while studying the Old Testament that I had the prophetic vision below. After stopping at Malachi, the last book before the New Testament, I wondered how the people of God could have complained with such ferocity and quickly forgotten the extraordinary, miraculous, and providential ways God had cared for them, century after century. I saw myself in studying these writings of Malachi. I had complained and had been so dismissive of His greatness in my own life. I had not loved Him with my whole heart, while I had loved other things and put them before God.

I must admit that I struggled with the whole issue of the godhead out of pure ignorance. The issue of the Spirit was the ultimate mystery, until I finally realized that without the third person of the Trinity, we were pretty much neutralized and living in the Dark Ages, without the power conduit through which God could work the miraculous. Thank God for the Cross and the blood of Jesus, which give us grace to all of our doubts and unbelief. Thank God for the nature of the godhead, right? The Lord emphatically states in Malachi that if Israel did not repent, she would be dealt with like the Edomites. I did not want to be dealt with as an Edomite, which would have been a curse forever. I repented on my knees again to lay my soul bare to God. I was ready to walk out of the desert and needed the water of life to fill the dryness. History bears understanding, lest we forget. How can we learn from mistakes if we do not know our past? My human cry, along with David's, is, "You, God, are my God, earnestly I seek you; I thirst for you, my whole being longs for you, in a dry and parched land where there is no water" (Psalm 63:1).

The Books of Promise: April 9, 2001

In this dream, my older daughter Tara and I were in a desert, traveling with thousands of women and children. It was like an exodus of sorts. We both had books under our arms (mine was large, hers smaller) as we led the way across the dry land. Our coats were tattered and torn from such a long and arduous journey; we had traveled for years. We were exhausted but had managed to keep the crowds of women moving through the desolate streets; we passed log fires burning in the ground. A swift runner, a young male messenger, came up to us on the dusty and forlorn road, much like an Olympian long-distance runner. How strange and inexplicable that his face was covered; I couldn't see from his thighs down. He ran shirtless while wearing a covering made out of a skin for modesty at his waist. This Olympian runner wore no shoes and had run for years, although he was not short of breath.

The message he delivered was urgent and one he had given along the way to many: "Get the women and children to the edge; this is the last day. Get them to the other side before destruction comes. Get out of this pillar area."

I had not noticed any pillar but became aware immediately that we were on the top of a flat surface. I was thinking how strange to be on a dais in the desert, but where was the edge? I was looking to where he pointed, and it seemed to be hundreds of miles over the horizon from the ledge we were on.

"Get out quickly," he reiterated forcefully as he ran on.

I wondered what kind of safety would we find somewhere past the edge of the world. I was neither frantic nor frustrated but sighed a little; it would take quite a while to herd this group. Obviously, from the size of our troupe, we were slow. We took his direction, and I was on high alert for any further mishaps along the road in the desert. Suddenly, there appeared an old shopping bazaar, much like you would see in biblical times. Middle Eastern hawkers under a palm tree were bellowing their wares. The structures holding each hanging product had been crudely made with sticks and roping wound together for strength. Like women from any country in the world, the massive group stopped to look at the materials for sale in the marketplace. We were all attracted to the long, flowing scarves made of gorgeous fabrics and hanging from wooden sticks that twirled. Every woman and child wanted to feel the lovely material they had missed seeing and wearing in our long journey. Vivid reds, purples, yellows, and blues were so beautiful and enticing compared to the dusty, dry neutrals of the desert veils and coats we had on. Where in the world had these tradesmen gotten the woven fabrics and array of colors? Everyone wanted to buy a scarf, but we had no money except the five dollars I carried in a little bag hanging from my belt. I was compelled to keep them moving on to reach the edge of the horizon on time. I remember thinking God was taking His time in getting us to the edge, if this was indeed the Last Day, as the runner had declared. Just as we reached the outer edge, fatigued but safe, we found an island we could rest on; it was called Seal Island. As we crossed over onto the island, the sky darkened and erupted in loud thunder and lightning in the distance. Had we missed the storm, or was it coming our way?

Seal Island, the Sanctuary: A Short Resting Place

The next scene opened into a large, ancient building, a church or maybe a synagogue. Paul was preaching a fiery sermon, but his clothes were striped pajama bottoms and a white T-shirt, not his usual pastoral garb. The church pews were packed with travelers. Most were oddly dressed in tattered pajamas, as if the nightclothes had been the only outerwear for years. Some travelers were wrapped in blankets to ward off the cold and damp air. We all looked like faded Holocaust survivors. I could just make out the images on the pajamas: stripes, flowers, and children's characters. A gentleman named Joe was standing on the right side of the pulpit while I stood at the left. Joe had a large envelope with prophetic words for people scribbled on scrap papers that he was pulling out of the envelope. I happened to see my name on two pieces. On one piece, my name was scribbled in pencil; on the other, it was in bold, black letters. I felt relieved when I saw him take it out, but he never gave it to me during the service.

As the sermon continued, there was a young boy sitting with his father on the left side of the congregation, close to where I stood. He spilled out into the aisle in an epileptic fit, but no one seemed alarmed. Paul did not stop preaching but caught my eye and nodded for me to take him out. It was the first time we had ever seen this happen in a church service. I helped the father gently carry the boy out of the aisle down into the ancient domed narthex. There was an old, worn wooden bench that fit snugly along the wall, as if it had been chiseled right into the stone. We used the bench to rest the young boy on and shivered from the chill.

Suddenly, the massive wooden front door was flung wide open from the outside. Some kind of event was taking place on the island beyond the horizon. It might have been the lightning and thunder I had seen and heard as we crossed onto the island. Beams of light were streaming through the door as a stocky, older gentleman stood in the portico and hurriedly announced that he was going to see what was over the horizon. He gave me a plan to meet up if we were separated. I didn't know this weathered little man, so I thought it odd that we should have a plan to rendezvous. Why had he even opened the door to the ancient church to tell me this?

After what seemed like an eternity, waiting with the boy and father sitting in the cold, damp narthex, he returned, but this time, the door was flung open with a such ferocious strength that it made me jump. I was shocked to see my new acquaintance's hair had completely turned white, like snow, and his clothes were disheveled. Had he been to the war front? It had been so long since he had left the church door. He had a very large leather book tucked under one arm that reminded me of a family Bible one might find in a museum.

The Declaration

His kindly eyes looked directly into mine across the old paved stoned floor as he bellowed from the doorway, "They have opened the Fifth Seal; they have opened the Fifth Seal. Get ready." I was shocked to hear this and sat very still on the wooden bench, trying to comprehend what the declaration might mean. His booming voice echoed in the domed narthex of the old church. With this last great declaration, I was released from the dream. I quickly jumped out of bed to run down to the living room and find my Bible. I felt there was no time to waste as I raced down the hall. I was wide awake from the jolt of my friend's booming voice and the nature of the dream.

What in the world does it say about the seals? I thought frantically. And what about this Fifth Seal in the Revelation of John? My hands visibly shook as I got to the couch and scanned through the opening chapters of Revelation. I did not have these events memorized. What did the angel of the Lord show him? Had I just seen the Ancient of Days depicted as God in the doorway? Was the book under this old man's arm the Lamb's Book of Life? I hurriedly ran through Revelation until my finger found the Fifth Seal spelled out. Here is what I read:

> *When he opened the fifth seal, I saw under the altar the souls of those who had been slain because of the word of God and the testimony they had maintained. They called out in a loud voice, "How long, Sovereign Lord, holy and true, until you judge the inhabitants of the earth and avenge our blood?" Then each of them was given a white robe, and they were told to wait a little longer, until the full number of their fellow*

> *servants, their brothers and sisters, were killed*
> *just as they had been.*

> *(Revelation 6:9–11)*

I sat, numb, for about a good five minutes after reading this passage. You will read about these great martyred servants once again in the last vision I have recorded in chapter 14. I had no idea that I would be introduced to them here and then several years later. My mind was racing like a tumultuous storm. Why was I given this dream? What was I to do with this? I read all the verses leading up to the seven seals and got so involved with the incredible destruction that I read on to the trumpets, which announce even more severe plagues than the seals. I then read every concordance reference on the end-times in a marathon, as I sat in contemplative thought waiting for the sun to rise in the early morning hours. The Fifth Seal had been opened leading up to the Apocalyptic last days and the perilous times the people of earth were about to experience from John's descriptive writings. Did John also sit in numbed silence on the Isle of Patmos as he received these incredible revelations from the angel of the Lord? I tried to put myself in his shoes. Were the times as bad as ours today in the twenty-first century, as he considered all that he had seen? Has the Fifth Seal been opened, and are we now awaiting the Age of the Trumpets to be sounded? All I want to proclaim at the moment is to get ready, church. Woe, woe, to the inhabitants of the earth.

Time to Reflect

1. What does the opening of the Fifth Seal mean to you?
2. Does this understanding of the Fifth Seal alter the way in which you might live out the rest of your life? Why?

Scripture Study

1. Read Matthew 24. Is God's grace sufficient for you to endure the end-times attack on the church of Christ?
2. Read Matthew 25. Assuming that you are a sheep, are you reflecting your vertical love for God as you horizontally respond to the needs of the people?

Chapter 10

The Fortress and the General

The Lord is my rock, my fortress and my deliverer; my God is my rock, in whom I take refuge, my shield and the horn of my salvation. He is my stronghold, my refuge and my savior— from violent people you save me.

—2 Samuel 22:2–3

David, the great warrior, was a conqueror, a shepherd, and a musician chosen to be the second king of Israel in the Old Testament. He was also a slayer of a bear, a lion, and the mammoth giant, Goliath. He was a good warrior, yes, but was he perfect? No. We are told, quite the opposite, on many occasions. He had fears, he had weaknesses in relationships and fatherhood, he murdered an innocent man, and oh, yes, like most of us, he despaired many times in his life, to the point of depression. But there is one solid vein of truth that ran through his crusty character.

He seemed to love and trust God. Scripture even tells us that God Himself declared that David was a man after His own heart. Where did this friendship come from, and how was it nurtured? Who would not want to personally be called someone after God's own heart? As a shepherd, I imagine he would have spent hours at night under the moonlight and stars: singing, maybe whistling softly to soothe his sheep to sleep, obviously talking to God, composing musical lyrics while protecting his flock as their responsible caregiver. He would have known what it was to have the safety of a fortress and for God to be his safety net out in the desert.

One evening at dusk, I was sitting lazily on one of our most favorite little beaches in Southport, Connecticut. The sun was just about down, and the waves rippled and lapped at the idyllic shoreline. I was thinking about King David and what it really meant for God to be his friend. I wanted the same kind of friendship with Jesus that he had. How peaceful and carefree to have this close of a relationship in order to talk and hang out in safety with the Creator. Obviously, the title of a sheepherder would not be on anyone's resume, except in the Middle East of today's modern world, but most humans can say they are drawn to the stars that circle our planet earth.

As a young girl, I remember being seduced by cool nights in my backyard tent. There was nothing better than lay out in the dewy evening on a blanket and watch the stars and wonder about the man in the moon. For just a brief moment on the beach, I closed my eyes to breathe in the beautiful autumn air and wondered if Jesus could really love me like David. It was there on the beach that Jesus brought me into His safety net to show me protection and to give me a vision of purpose and destiny. In this vision, I was going to see a partial window into the calling that God was giving Paul and me.

Fall 2002 Vision

In this vision on a beach in Connecticut, I was maybe eight or nine years old, skipping up to a path of stones through a forest. Pebbles were stacked neatly along the landscaped winding path, with wildflowers and foliage peeking out between gaps of stone leading somewhere into the deep forest. I was alone and young, but I was not thinking about being lost. Shortly thereafter, I happened upon an immense, ancient fortress, looming in the middle of the forest. It was a little shocking to see such a massive fort in the rocky pathway. The gigantic wooden gates were thickly hewn and flung open wide in front of me. At least forty chiseled iron nails were hammered into each door that I could see. I looked up above the fortress and could see a large cast iron bell hung securely in the majestic belfry. There was a long dangling rope knotted at the top of the bell, and for one short second, I wished I could hear the sound of this great bell; if only there was someone there to pull the cord.

A man who was standing in the massive door called out softly, "Come up here to me." He was the most beautiful man I had ever seen. Somehow, I knew it was Jesus. He stood in the entrance in a simple, splendid white robe with a rope belt. I remember his eyes were pure pools of love that reached out to beckon me up behind the thick walls of the mighty fortress. I wanted to climb right up into His lap, but we were both standing at the moment. What a silly thought. Certainly, we had just met. As I walked through the door, I glanced over my shoulder and watched as the great Christ Himself pulled the heavy iron lever down to lock the wooden gate in its secure trough. We were somewhere off of planet earth, standing on the edge of the universe. I could see a sea of grass before us like a verdant pasture, spreading for hundreds of miles in the distance. Beyond that distance and over the edge, I saw the sphere of planet earth exactly like the epic photographs I had seen snapped by our astronauts from outer space. Whatever this all meant from the vortex of where forest and fortress met, it was beautiful to observe where I had once lived on planet earth.

How odd, but I looked down at my clothes, and I was no longer a young child but a young woman. At this astonishing discovery, I felt Jesus gently wrap me in a long purple cloth from my head to toe. He called me by name and told me He loved me as He twirled me around in the gorgeous royal fabric. Once again, an incredible feeling of freedom and security washed over me, as pure love touched me with His words and His actions. I happened to turn to my left side and squinted into the far distance and saw what looked like a low row of stables dotting the horizon. There seemed to be enough stables for hundreds of horses.

Stealth Strength

From the stables, I saw four separate doors open, and four monstrous white stallions with wings bolted out of their stalls and thundered toward us. It was much like the Kentucky Derby when the gates open and the Thoroughbreds start the race. Each horse had a red blanket but no saddle on its back. The red blanket did not flap in the wind but was secured by an unseen force, holding it down. What I was most struck by were the horses' ice blue eyes that I could see, even as they thundered toward us from hundreds of miles away. They were fierce and intently focused on their mission. Where in the world were they going? I held my breath and was overwhelmed by the vast space across the grassy knoll they were galloping through. I could hear their hooves beating firmly along the ground and could feel the booming sound under my feet.

As they closed in on Jesus and me, I could see their nostrils flaring from the wind and wondered if they would run us over. I was staggered by their sheer strength and aware that each mighty muscle of these magnificent animals was rippling under the skin. These were no ordinary stallions. These were the kings of their breed and almost supernatural. All four came to a stop in front of Jesus, without a speck of dust in their wake. They had run so far, but none of them were short of breath or streaked with sweat on their spotless white coats. I cannot remember ever seeing white like this particular shade of white on any animal.

The General

A man of great stature came into the vision from our right side and strolled confidently toward us. He was an ancient soldier of some kind by the markings on his clothing. Maybe a general or official, I thought. His silver helmet had a stately red plume attached to the top, and it was waving as if there was a breeze, which I did not feel. The steel visor was shut, but I could see the man's eyes peering through the grates of the helmet. What? Did I see a hint of familiarity of my husband's eyes hidden behind those grates? I am not quite sure, but I felt as if he might be staring a hole right through me. The extraordinary steel breastplate he wore was encrusted with large gemstones: emeralds, sapphires, amethysts, rubies, diamonds, and pearls. Simple but magnificently placed in square and organized lines across his chest, which might have been worn by a high priest from biblical times. The sandals he wore had leather straps beautifully woven to the knee, which emphasized this man's strong muscular thighs. I knew then with a certainly that this was Paul, my husband, because of those legs. I was a little embarrassed in front of Jesus by this discovery.

Destiny Calls

Jesus stood between us with a beautiful little girl in His arms. I knew her name was Rachel, although she had not been introduced to me. He put Rachel on the red blanket in the middle of the four stallions, while the mighty warrior came around and took my right foot to help me mount the second steed. Before he mounted his great white stallion, Jesus pointed to planet earth beyond the space of green miles of where we were standing. This time, I saw the earth suspended on its axis in space, with a steel stake running through the earth from north to south with a beautiful white blanket, which looked much like ice cream, melting from the North Pole to the South and touching the equator with jagged tips. There were also two wide steel bands, which encircled and reinforced the earth's equator from the east and west.

The mighty warrior next to me mounted his stallion, and Jesus signaled with His right arm and said, "Go; it is yours. Speak the truth."

I knew we were going to conquer something on this major quest but did not know what we were doing. It was not an adventure we were on but a mission of purpose and life. There was no doubt that it was going to be a conquest with the great general by my side. We had one another; we had Jesus, and we did have our directive.

After I was released from this vision, I felt a tremendous burden lifted from my shoulders. Jesus was my rock and my salvation, and there was nothing I would ever fear, as long as I was in His care. I loved the visual of Jesus pulling the bar down on the doors, as if to reassure me there would be no siege to take us out of His safe refuge. How refreshing to note that we are safe and sound with Jesus and will always be protected from our enemies.

I hope you had this same reflection of your own life in the care of the Master. You are safe. I also felt that Paul as a warrior and general knew how to take the land for Christ and that God was showing us a mission of taking the earth in strength (the stallions) and in a path of wisdom. With the mantel of high priest, I believe he will apostolically oversee many parts of the mission we are to take. I am still not sure what the great steel bands mean. Did the four white horses denote power of direction to the north, south, east, and west? I am on a mission, praying to find the answer.

Time to Reflect

1. Where do you turn for help when the bottom is falling out?
2. When the going gets tough, do you trust in your own strength or in Jesus?

Scripture Study

1. Read Philippians 4:10–13. What advice does St. Paul give when going through difficult times?
2. Read 1 Kings 17:2–16. How did God provide for His own? Do you believe He can do the same for you?

Chapter 11

Taken to Heaven

*I have seen you in the sanctuary and beheld
your power and your glory. Because your love
is better than life, my lips will glorify you. I will
praise you as long as I live, and in your name I
will lift up my hands. I will be fully satisfied as
with the richest of foods; with singing lips my
mouth will praise you.*

—Psalm 63:2–5

June 12 had never been an ordinary day on the
calendar for Paul and me. We were married on this date,
and in celebrating our anniversary, we always thought of
unique ways to make it a special memory. Our twenty-fifth
wedding anniversary was obviously a very big milestone
in marriage. We had made it to this pivotal point of our
relationship, through thick and thin. We were deciding
what we should do when Paul learned there were thirty

pastors and ministry leaders meeting in New Jersey for a monthly luncheon. Robert Stearns, who is a dear friend in ministry and who we had met in Baltimore that famous prophetic weekend, led worship and Bible study at these meetings. Paul had wanted to attend one of these for some time to connect with other leaders in the tri-state area.

It just happened that on June 12, 2003, a luncheon had been scheduled, and Paul asked me if I would like to drive over to New Jersey for this luncheon. After the initial shock of Paul suggesting that we attend a pastor's meeting on our anniversary, Mr. Romantic quickly asserted he would take us to a beautiful dinner in New York City afterwards. We would not have to travel too far from New Jersey, as New York was right across the Hudson River, connecting the two states. My life would again be turned upside down as I was taken to a new spiritual level this particular day. God certainly had an extraordinary anniversary surprise waiting for us.

We drove that morning from Connecticut to a magnificent Victorian mansion where the pastors were meeting. In its heyday, I imagine the old commuter neighborhood was one of the loveliest streets in America. I remembered the beautiful gardens that surrounded this enchanting home perched on a hill and the antiques that adorned the interiors. After introductions were made, we stepped down into the grand living room, where I also imagined large galas had taken place over the years. Worship began promptly at ten o'clock.

Stephen Jenks, Robert's accompanist, hit the perfectly

pitched ivory keys on the black lacquered grand piano. The musical notes seemed to dance over the keyboard and filled the great room like a concert hall. I've never heard such a resonant sound from a solo keyboard as this and thought it might have sounded a little heavenly, with the instrument harmonizing with the soaring men's voices in baritone and tenor notes. My last conscious memory was a small, hand-carved statue of the Israelites carrying the Ark of the Covenant sitting atop the library table, behind the couch I was standing in front of.

I closed my eyes to listen to the men worship, and that was the last thing I remember seeing, as my whole body was taken up in a shaft of light, much like a express elevator. Was the speed of light like this? The ark on the back of the table and the earth were left hundreds of miles away, in what seemed like a few seconds. The elevator stopped somewhere in the solar system, but I never saw or heard a door open or close behind me. I was in some sort of a glorious sea of space I had never visited before, and for a split-second, while regaining my bearings, I do remember thinking three words as if in slow motion: *Oh, my goodness.* One thing I absolutely recall was the feeling of an encompassing presence of safety and perfect peace, which permeated my entire body. I felt no fear at all, just security. Fear was not of this place.

I know I must have stood in shock for a moment, eventually realizing that I was standing in a massive space called heaven. Profound love like ribbons encircled me as the realization settled in. Love, love, love in every square inch surrounded me and oozed into every pore of my body. It was circling and dancing around my head, arms, legs, and feet. Could pure love even be seen? What is it, anyway? It is almost impossible to articulate in human language, but what I can equate it to is that of a newborn baby being laid in one's arms for the first time. A holy reverence overtakes many mothers when they meet their child for the first time outside of the womb. I know it did mine when they were brought into the world. No wonder the angels sang the glorious "Hallelujah" at the birth of Jesus as He was laid in Mary's arms. They were giving homage to the magnificent glory of God, Who would be our pure light of the world and love magnet for all to come to.

As I stood in the midst of this sterile pureness, the strength of white light, initially like thousands of megawatt light bulbs, blinded me. It took a minute to adjust to the brilliance, but I suddenly looked down and realized I was standing on a glassy street made of pure gold. It was just as I had read about in the book of Revelation. I had never seen such mirrored beauty in the shimmery gold mixed into the glass. I could not see where the street started or ended, but in the next instant, I knew God was surrounding me where I stood. As incredible as it sounds, I was in the throne room of God; it felt as if I had always been there.

He encircled me like a cocoon filled with the most incredible love, wrapping me up from head to toe, but not tightly. God was not in a human form sitting on the throne but an omnipotent force field, taking up the vastness of space, which surrounded me. Rolling waves of love came in wave after wave to hem me in. His face was next to mine. We were nose to nose. Had I ever been so close to anyone as I was with God, nose to nose? I didn't think there was any space between us. While we were nose to nose, red rays of fire pierced through my soul and spirit. His blazing red eyes penetrated right through my eyes like laser beams. I was spellbound in His presence. A new sensation of life coursed through every nerve ending, almost like all systems in my body were on go or high alert, but peaceful and not at all hyper. He and I were together, alone, and yet we were one. I felt as if I had been with this awesome presence from the beginning of time. He was not a stranger to me, which was a consoling thought at the incredible moment. Had I died and gone to heaven?

I had had so many questions to ask of God, but quite frankly, those questions never came to mind where I stood. All was forgotten and seemed inconsequential and trivial to think about. Time was irrelevant in this vast heavenly system. He saw and knew all about me. At some point, I remember peeking around His great form, or maybe He allowed me to take in the scene because I was able to see His actual throne. The image of the immense throne took my breath away. Did He hear my breath suck in as I tried to comprehend the size? Maybe He smiled through the light of presence, but I can only estimate the size of the throne to be about ten thousand football fields in length and width. There were grand steps leading up to the top of the mystical pure white stage. Having only seen the velvets and brocades of European throne rooms in castle tours, I was not quite sure what God's chair might have looked like. Don't be concerned about having enough room for us all to fit into the heavenly realm. There is room there for billions of souls. From my vantage point, size will not be an issue, as long as we are with our King. He bent from His waist down to my eye level from the throne and gently wrapped His Fatherly fingers around my chin, which He lifted with such gentleness and said, "I love you, Rivers."

Ah! He knew my name. His heavenly voice was velvet; it was beauty and majesty, all wrapped into one. His next statement did take me by surprise, if one can feel surprise in heaven, but conversation was flowing.

God said to me gently, "I never asked for the gift that I gave to you. I never asked for it back."

I immediately knew the Father was addressing the gift of my singing voice. I had bargained with Him twenty-two years earlier when Paul II nearly died after falling out the apartment window. At the time, I thought the bargaining chip was my voice and the desire to be on an operatic stage, singing famous roles for sopranos. The bargain that I made with God was that if He would save our little boy, I would stop singing. God was not angry nor reprimanding me about the bargain I had made, but standing before Him in this realm, I realized I had lived without a song in my heart for all those empty years. The creative void my soul had grieved for and found in the ancient artisans while traveling in Rome had stirred a deep desire in that cavernous hole.

I realized without guilt or shame that God had created us all in such detail to be in union with Him and had lavishly gifted humankind for His delight in all of the creative arts and more. Had we lost it? I certainly had. With our gifted accomplishment, it was also for the divine accomplishment of our Father that He vigorously relished all of us to succeed and to love our gifts. He had given me my voice as a gift, but I had given it away, however innocent it had been done at the time. After looking back over this incredible experience in the third heaven, I also understood why sniveling Satan enjoys stealing. Of course, he is the ultimate thief. Why would the evil one want anyone to sing or speak of the glory of the Lord?

Jesus and the Heavenly Beings

As I stood basking in love, another surprise awaited me. I glanced to my right, and the beautiful Christ appeared next to me. He was not a spirit but in the form I remembered having seen from pictures. I was standing shoulder to shoulder with the most stunning and handsome Jesus that no artist had ever captured with pen or brush. His eyes melded into mine with such love and compassion that it took my breath away again. I could see the fine woven linen garment He wore and a beautiful gold sash, which encircled His waist. Jesus instructed me to follow the direction of His right arm, which seemed eternally long, strong, and with incredibly smooth skin hidden under the sleeve of the robe. If I were to close my eyes today, I would still be able to identify the skin on His beautiful hands.

I followed Jesus's right arm as far as I could see in the vast space of heaven and saw millions upon millions of the strangest-looking creatures I've ever seen. Following His strong arm to the left were just as many of these ET-looking creatures. Oddly, all were dressed alike in what seemed to be a whitish-gray robe of some kind. I could not see below the thigh area. They had no noses, but they did have large round eyes and round mouths with larger heads. I guess they didn't need to smell in heaven. The sense of smell never invaded the atmosphere for me to remember or write down in my dream journal. All of these creatures to the right and left were singing in unison using notes that were incomparable and nearly indescribable. It was Apocalyptic at best. Can you imagine how extraordinary and epic a scene it was to not only hear millions of voices, but to see the vast numbers with only mouths moving in unison? Humanly speaking, I had never heard such glorious notes like this chorus of inestimable numbers, which sounded like tinkling glass bells. Music was coming through the bells in such a way that all of heaven's space was filled with voices. If this was glory, then I had discovered the mysterious definition.

Time seemed unnecessary in the spatial paradise where serenity, peace, and the Word existed. That was it; the Word was God, and His Kingdom shall have no end, and in His dominion, we shall live for eternity with no time constraints. A stunning thought for earth's inhabitants.

The Rays of Beams

I do not know if God ushered me to another spacious room as large as the one I was in, or if the scene changed to include the altar, but there was an incredible light show taking place around the altar. Much like the northern lights I witnessed in Iceland, the beams were incredible dancing rays as wide as skyscrapers.

In each beam, there were trillions and trillions of colored gemstones. I looked into outer space above heaven to see if any of the beams ever ended. They did not. One ray was filled with sapphires, while the next with rubies, one with pearls the size of large buildings, another with diamonds, the next with emeralds, the next with sapphires, and another with amber. I chuckled to think I figured out where all of our lost jewelry and stones must go. Of course, that is total conjecture on my part, if not just a nice thought. However, the beams were incredible as they danced around the spectacular altar.

It was several years later when Jeff Williams, a Lutheran astronaut we met at a NASA conference, came to our church to give his testimony of faith and a remarkable presentation on his personal walk in space. As part of his scientific presentation, he included extraordinary footage of NASA spacecraft orbiting Earth. From the professional video, we learned that every ninety minutes, the world rotates or orbits from complete darkness into stark light from the sun. The epiphany came that weekend as I searched for the answer to the rays of beams. The footage captured the spacecraft coming out of complete darkness into the daylight, and for half of a split-second, the fan-shaped, multicolored beams burst onto the horizon to announce the day. Bingo. The rays dancing around the altar praising God might just be the same beams filled with the brilliance of the stones to glorify God in the daylight. I hope explained that well enough for you to research the atmosphere and its beauty.

After the light show, I wanted to stay in heaven forever. I never wanted to leave the safety of God's presence. He read my mind, of course, and gently told me it was not yet time to stay and that I must go back to earth. In what had seemed like hours, I was released from the incredible vision of the third heavenly realm. My eyes closed, and then they opened, and I want to think that maybe death is a little like this sensation while we wait for God and the Last Day. Time seemed to have no limitations, no beginning, and no end, but I remember that God did not say goodbye, either.

I absolutely did not want to open my eyes. Where was I? Ah. I came back to reality. I opened my eyes, and there I stood, as I had when Stephen had touched the ivory keys in the great living room of the Victorian mansion. I was in New Jersey. I think I pinched myself to see if I was alive.

I was still standing in front of the couch, but now every fiber of my body was quivering. My blood was coursing through my body, and I was trying to see if it felt like fire or ice. I was shaking from within and from head to toe, as one would shake from a high fever. However, tranquility invaded me, although the fire did not leave me for at least several hours.

As I opened my eyes, I also saw the pastors and a missionary from India lying on the floor, weeping loudly. My mind had to quickly readjust and comprehend all that had just taken place. It was surreal. Paul slowly got up and came over to me by the front of the couch and told me I had been singing to them. I was momentarily confused by what he told me because I had not felt my own vocal cords utter a sound while away with God. It would have been awesome to have some kind of recording made that morning. I would have treasured the new song God had given me in my heart. He had also given me the most extraordinary anniversary gift I could ever receive, and it was from God to both Paul and to me. Like many scriptures that attest to goodness, He had lavished on me His perfect love and power in a display of wonder and splendor in a place called heaven. How could anything be better than that?

If you might remember from several stories I have woven in this book, I had a horrible fear of death, dying, darkness, and hospitals. I was excruciatingly affected by the death of the little girl murdered in Philadelphia, our son's fall in Japan, and the crisis both of my brothers faced as toddlers. God knew I needed to see that heaven was for real and that He had me lovingly in His care. I could finally achieve healing in knowing with confidence that I was safe with God and free from fear that had gripped my mind for such a long time. It was utterly merciful of Him to give me such an extravagant gift of pure truth to calm my fears.

As for you, go with God and serve Him with all of your heart, your soul, and your might. Because of this profound healing, may you too have a new song put into your heart like mine. The psalmist expressed it beautifully in Psalm 40:3: "He put a new song in my mouth, a hymn of praise to our God. Many will see and fear and put their trust in the Lord."

Time to Reflect

1. When you contemplate crossing over the threshold of death, do you face these thoughts with fear or peace?
2. Is heaven real?

Scripture Study

1. Read John 14:25–29. What role does the Holy Spirit play in helping you face death?
2. Read 1 Thessalonians 4:4–17. As a believer in Jesus, do you think He will ever forget you?

Chapter 12

The African Beauty

I had a farm in Africa.

—*Karen Blixen, Out of Africa*

September was a time when Paul and I got away and used a few weeks before school started as a time of prayer, fasting, and entreaty of the Lord. We were asking God in this new season of our lives for His strategy, direction, and revelation for our dear church and for the people God was sending to us in Westport. Every year, if schedules allowed, a dear couple from the church, Bridget and Greg, gave us their little cottage on the Cape in Massachusetts to relax and recoup before the busy fall season. This particular September in 2004 was no different. The Cape was a magical place where no two sunsets on the wide horizon are ever alike. It was also a serene getaway, where the laziness of cloud formations roll by and where one can sit out at night under millions of stars to watch planets sparkle brilliantly on the coastal beach. You get the picture. It was a paradise for any couple wanting to rest and sleep with the ebbing tides lapping on the rocks below our bedroom windows.

In 2004, our church leadership also voted to fast with us during our time there. We had an arsenal of strength in numbers back home and could actually feel the power building each day as we went before the Lord in entreaty before the Cross. Sometimes, I felt it could have been Mount Horeb, where Moses spent time with the Lord for his people, the Israelites. Secretly, I did check to see if Paul's hair had turned white on any of the mornings as he came off the mountain with God. We worshipped about an hour with music and then went into intense prayer that varied in length each day. Paul would sit in an overstuffed chair, and I would lay on the couch with my eyes closed, head propped up on the arm of the couch. Each day, I was taken into deep visions during this prayer time. My experiences varied: walking on the beach with Jesus or just sitting in a quiet garden surrounded by roses and other flowers. These visions were healing to my soul for various reasons, but God whispered love and peace to me and strategy to Paul. On the third day after our Bible study and intercession, a profound feeling of unity intensified, as if God was pouring out incredible power from heaven over my entire body.

One of my favorite Hollywood movies is *Out of Africa*, with Meryl Streep and Robert Redford. Meryl played Karen Blixen in the epic film about Africa. What a remarkable trailblazer and historical pioneer woman she was, to pull up exotic roots from Europe and leave for Africa to forge her way into a coffee business. Blixen was someone I could personally identify with as a pioneer. In one of the first scenes of the classic movie, the train makes its long, slow winding journey across the Serengeti. I always close my eyes during this scene and am transfixed by the romance, the intrigue, and the haunting music of Africa. It is a fragrant reminder of a land so diverse with the humorous and quirky animals of God, the tribal peoples of His creation, and their peculiar traditions and cultural habits. Why did God create Africa for the world? I have asked myself this question on several occasions.

Paul and I have made over fourteen mission, conference, and crusade trips to African nations, each teaching us more about the people, the cultures, and the traditions. We experienced and ministered to the diversity of needs, plight, and poverty. We have seen the barrenness and the abundance and marveled at how countries like this could have incredible natural resources and yet be so poor in body, spirit, and economical poverty. We have worked with leaders and have seen what corruption and cruelty can do to thwart the growth of a nation for centuries. We have also seen the witch doctors and their entourage work in village after village, fueling superstitions that haunt the trusting public.

And then there are the precious children, the vulnerable orphaned street children who are addicted to glue and assorted drugs that thwart the hunger pains.

These children are toddlers and teens who live in squalor under trees, homemade shanties of cardboard, and highway underpasses, where no one cares for them. As you might know, there are orphaned communities by the thousands in every African nation. They live on meager provisions while begging for day-old bread and sparse rations. Most try to survive, and that's about the length of their short life, which is overwhelmed by such sheer deficiency.

Here is the truth: The people of Africa have been raped by the world. I get overwhelmed myself just thinking of all we have seen in brokenness and pitiful situations. How do they manage in the era of AIDS and mosquito-driven diseases, droughts, high mortality rates, famines, and the massacre of war? One morning close to the end of our trip, the Spirit of God led me and Paul to Africa in a vision.

Cape Cod, Massachusetts 2004 Vision

A tree cannot stand on the ground without its roots.

—African proverb

Paul and I were standing on a majestic plateau in Africa. An ancient acacia tree stood to his left, and two beautiful lions, male and female, were seated in close proximity to us in the clear daylight. The lion is one of the stateliest beasts in the African wilds. The male's mane was like a crown encircling the head of the king of the jungle; his eyes were alert but calm. The sleek female to my right gazed intently out over the throngs of people in front of the plateau. She seemed to be waiting for something to happen. I wanted to touch her to feel her sinewy power. Their tails twitched in the soft, hot breeze.

Both Paul and I were dressed in white. Paul wore a starched white shirt and slacks. He was strong, tanned, and a man of integrity. I had such respect for him. I looked to him for guidance, knowing that he waited on God with such great faith, patience, and absolute trust in listening to God to make his next strategic moves. We had worked diligently side by side in Africa. I wore a long, flowing kaftan dress with a white headdress. I could not see our shoes in the vision; maybe we were barefoot. We were gazing intently over the plains, where millions of Africans stood before us, a plethora of color in deeply rich blacks and cognac browns. Each person in the vision was dressed in glorious costumes of tribal tradition. The sea of color was breathtaking to the eye, which was such a contrast next to their skin color. The throngs were softly singing lyrical African melodies in native tongues, and while they sang and hummed, they would sway to the rhythm. It was a majestic and spectacular scene to drink in. This all reminded me of the great multitude in white robes I have read about in the book of Revelation:

> *After this I looked, and there before me was*
> *a great multitude that no one could count,*
> *from every nation, tribe, people and language,*
> *standing before the throne and before the Lamb.*
> *They were wearing white robes and were holding*
> *palm branches in their hands.*

> *(Revelation 7:9)*

In the next scene, Paul and I were giving Communion to the masses, but no one seemed to be in a rush or hurry to get to us. I was struck by how peacefully they made their way to the bottom of the plateau for the Lord's Supper, as if they truly relished this very holy moment in freedom. They had once been enemies, but now something was different. As Communion was distributed to those who stood before us, Paul periodically raised his outstretched arms to the throngs, as if praying a father's blessing over them and over Africa, their homeland.

From the left side of the vision, as far as I could see, there were thousands upon thousands of soldiers present from every nation on the African continent. Whole platoons were dressed in varying combinations of greens and brown army fatigues and filing silently forward to lay their rifles and machine guns down to take Communion. The guns were piled in enormous mounds at the bottom of the plateau below us. The soldiers were not in a surrendering posture, I noticed, but more like war had been declared over, and they were absolutely exhausted from it all. They wanted something different now. Peace and unity was what they yearned for. I could see the desire in their eyes and sense the way their shoulders slumped in weariness.

Suddenly, without any warning, a massive python with a gigantic head came slithering from the top of the vision and slowly swirled about our feet, ready to strike and suffocate us. As swift as the python had appeared, a gigantic foot came into the entire scene and stomped on the head to crush it. I knew immediately it was the foot of Jesus. I could only see the bottom of His white robes and His burly sandaled foot, but I was now well acquainted with the Master and the way He moved. His powerful foot destroyed the beast in a dramatic finish, once and for all. Thankfully, I was never terrified of this python, as I would have been in the natural. My faith and trust in God were strong and resilient, and I knew without a doubt that God would come in for the strategic strike at just the right time.

Immediately following the instant death of the snake, the most beautiful notes of music began to waft from the crowds at the back. I peered down to our right side of the African beauties and saw delicate white maidens far in the distance, coming toward the plateau; they were making their way over the miles. Each delicate dancer had fair skin, blonde hair, and flowers encircling their curled tresses. I could see the turquoise blue of their eyes while the white creaminess of their skin caught my immediate attention. They were wearing long, white flowing gowns of gossamer chiffon, embellished with flowing ribbons, which was one of my favorite fabrics for a ball. They were dancing, singing, and praising God with flutes, and they were the most beautiful dancing handmaidens I had ever seen. Their movements were so delicate and light, like prima ballerinas. A panoramic scene was then opened that showed all the entities of the vision, which included the lions, the tree, the masses, and the angelic dancers who worshipped with Paul and me on the plateau. The peace of God settled over us all.

I was lifted out of the formidable African vision. Although it was a short vision, I believe there was relevance to what I was being shown concerning the continent and its people. It was comforting to know that one day, Africa would be unified under the blood of the Lamb and the body of Christ; it was reassuring that a continent who had been under centuries of such tyranny, pillage, and rape would be set free, the colonial powers trampled. I like the word *trample*. It denotes strength and finality. God trampled the enemies of His people in the Old and New Testament and gives us the right to do the same in the power of the Spirit. There might be much more to this interpretation. I am searching.

Jesus said, "I saw Satan fall like lightning from heaven. I have given you authority to trample on snakes and scorpions and to overcome all the power of the enemy; nothing will harm you. However, do not rejoice that the spirits submit to you, but rejoice that your names are written in heaven" (Luke 10:18–20).

Time to Reflect

The victory will always belong to the Lord.

1. Do you believe Jesus Christ has conquered Satan, the world, death, the grave, sin, and hell?
2. Do you believe in your heart and mind that the victory of Christ over all these things are applicable to you? Or are you still uncertain?

Scripture Study

1. Read Matthew 16:17–19. Do you believe that Satan will not be able to prevail against you because of Jesus Christ?
2. Read Revelation 12:9–13. What is your defense against Satan?

Chapter 13

The Beverly Hills Hilton Hotel

"This is Hollywood, my dear."

Los Angeles is a town abuzz with traffic jams, movie moguls, famous names engraved on corporate skyscrapers, star sightings, decadence, and a who's who of sex, glamour, and dreams for those aspiring to be famous in one way or the other. Most people who live outside the Hollywood bubble agree it is a city full of emptiness and faux hearts, blocked hearts, broken hearts, empty hearts, lost hearts, faint of heart, and sold-out hearts. All seem so frail as hearts go. Many also believe that it is the faux capital of an industry of fantasy, pretentiousness, and predators.

I recently found two passages that speak to the heart of the matter as I reflected on the reputation of Tinsel Town. The first concerns the prophet Jeremiah, who asks a rhetorical question on the state of the heart: "The heart is deceitful above all things and beyond cure.

183

Who can understand it? 'I the Lord search the heart and examine the mind, to reward each person according to their conduct, according to what their deeds deserve'" (Jeremiah 17:9–10). The second is from King Solomon, who brings admonition to a wise son: "My son, pay attention to what I say; turn your ear to my words. Do not let them out of your sight, keep them within your heart; for they are life to those who find them and health to one's whole body. Above all else, guard your heart, for everything you do flows from it. Keep your mouth free of perversity; keep corrupt talk far from your lips. Let your eyes look straight ahead; fix your gaze directly before you. Give careful thought to the paths for your feet, and be steadfast in all your ways. Do not turn to the right or the left; keep your foot from evil" (Proverbs 4:20–27).

Here is where the story of a hotel begins and how God showed me a most incredible revelation through a dream. Maybe the handwriting on the wall concerned the heart of the matter upon which the city of Los Angeles struggles.

It all began in the spring of 2003, while planning the eighty-fifth birthday party for our pastor-at-large, Harald Bredesen, who lived in San Diego. The birthday committee, as they were known, thought it easier for Harald to celebrate on the West Coast, where many of his friends lived. I was a part of this volunteer committee and had flown out to LA from Connecticut to research several hotels and the feasibility of renting a large enough space to honor Harald for his work with various world leaders for international peace. We all decided that his momentous occasion should be located in LA to handle the growing numbers of interested invitees. I had five hotels on my list to visit as possibilities. At the first hotel, I met Denny Fitzpatrick, the general manager of the Beverly Hills Hilton Hotel (BHHH). He personally took me on a tour after our initial introduction and became more excited about the event as we talked about what we wanted to accomplish. He had heard of Harald Bredesen from years past and really thought the Hilton would be the proper venue for this esteemed man of God. After interviewing all five hotel event managers, making the right decision was easier for me when the Hilton offered its famous international ballroom for his special evening.

I believed that after the initial interview with the general manager, he carried a mantle of extraordinary qualities as an executive leader in the hotel industry. During our tour, I learned that he was about to undertake a rigorous renovation of the older hotel. On many subsequent visits, I watched as he generously opened his office door to employees or visitors who needed prayer or to any groups that wanted to pray for the BHHH because of its standing in the city. Paul and I personally called Denny "the cheerleader for the kingdom of God" and are fast friends until eternity. He was and is still today an encourager for the countless people who cross his path and need spirits lifted and prayer requests fulfilled. I would call him an extraordinary friend of God. In addition to his stellar character in the workplace, he was a record-breaking college quarterback for the University of Washington in his college days, so maybe *cheerleader* is the wrong word to describe him. Had I not chosen this exact hotel in 2003, I would not have had Denny as a dear friend, and I would not have heard from God in a most extraordinary way.

My volunteer job was to give a report of the progress to the committee, which I promptly did. Quite frankly, I had no idea how I got roped into the celebration so directly, but I took the assignment seriously and wanted to help make this special event a monumental affair for Harald. Anyone who has ever planned an event knows that it just does not happen without a lot of headaches and stress. As one volunteer aptly quipped, "This is Hollywood, my dear. We do it differently out here." Well, I guess they did do it differently. Hollywood appears to do everything outside the box, and this was going to be one of those events. I quickly learned it was more work than I bargained for. Everyone wanted to be the event planner on volunteer status, and everyone wanted to be comped free for the dinner (Hollywood's gratuity for fame). I learned a lot about the culture of the town during the few short months to pull the party together. Fortunately, it turned out to be a grand affair, but God had the last word in why He wanted me in Los Angeles. It was for a totally different purpose than I first thought.

The Beverly Hilton itself has a glamorous history, which stands on its own merits. It is located at the intersection of Wilshire and Santa Monica Boulevards in Beverly Hills, California. During her time as a hotel icon of Hollywood, the venue has hosted hundreds of awards shows, charitable benefits, and events for the rich and famous. It is most famously known for its glitzy annual event called the Golden Globe Awards and Oscar luncheons with the full weight of the ever-encroaching paparazzi. For years, it was owned by the famous entertainer and producer, Merv Griffin, and remains a bedazzling icon to the entertainment industry. Most who know this historical edifice would say it was one of Hollywood's oldest and finest. Thankfully, I was able to eat in the famous Trader Vic's restaurant before it was demolished, but in the fall of 2003, Paul and I were there once more to visit our friend Denny and to debrief the event while praying for the city and hotel.

I had stopped earlier that morning at the airport shop in New York before boarding the flight to the West Coast and purchased a notebook for the trip. I happened to select one with a beautiful lighthouse on the front cover, for the only reason that Paul II loved to sketch lighthouses when he was younger. When we stepped into Denny's office that afternoon, he had a large lighthouse on his desk he had just been given, and we quipped at how strange it was we both had a lighthouse motif going for our California trip. We all agreed the rest we needed those few days would be helpful and joked that we would catch up on our news during Denny's breaks late at night. He had slept in the hotel for months because he needed to be nearby due to issues during the multimillion-dollar renovation. In actuality, he had not had time to find an affordable living arrangement in the LA area to be close to his position at the hotel.

At Denny's invitation, we chose to stay in the very famous hotel cabana rooms by the pool, only because we wanted a different hotel experience, and why not? I had seen these cabana rooms in so many movies and poolside interviews before. Settling down after dinner the first night, I do believe it was totally ordained by God to be on the West Coast with Denny while enjoying a perfectly spectacular and cloudless Sunday evening with each other in the iconic hotel. While relaxing by the pool under the moonlight and listening to the rustling leaves of the great palm trees, the Pacific breeze brushed over our faces. We decided that there might not be a more spectacular spot in the world. With that lingering thought, we were exhausted from the time change and went to sleep in our little cabana by the pool.

During the night, I had an incredible prophetic dream, which I have labeled several components as an easier way for you to follow:

The Finger of God

It was an early but lazy evening; we were sitting by the pool under the shade of a large cabana umbrella at the Beverly Hills Hilton Hotel. The few stately palm trees were gently waving in the cool breeze. I was talking with a friend from Los Angeles visiting me at the hotel, a Jewish movie producer. I do not remember how the subject of abortion came up in our conversation, but we both agreed that it was imperative that a Hollywood movie should be made in giving the unborn a vital voice in our society. Why should they not have a voice? They were simply maturing in their first home, the womb, to be born to speak. Our chairs were facing toward the back of the hotel, overlooking the pool, with the giant stucco wall to our right. (You know exactly where we were sitting if you have seen photos of the famous hotel.) My friend was adamantly opposed to the destruction of babies for the purpose of convenience and believed, as I, that it was murder of a human being who had all inalienable rights of personhood.

He was keen on the idea of producing this film, and I passionately agreed with his direction and wanted desperately to do something to jar the moral compass of America. What was wrong with our society in giving hearty approval to murder? Our conversation involved many aspects on the subject of life that he wanted to accomplish in writing the script to this movie. In the dream, I was more of an advisor to this timely script. As our conversation became more involved and intense, we happened to gaze up at the back of the hotel, which was facing the pool area and alight with the brilliant sun from the west. There were ten or so floors with draped windows and iron railings, which marked each balcony along the floors. We looked and watched in silence as a massive finger was writing something between each floor. Of course, we were shocked and sat speechless and riveted as the finger scrolled onto the concrete stone between each floor and spilled out onto the stucco wall to the right. As the finger wrote, my Jewish friend whispered that he recognized the following words written in Hebrew: "YHVH, Jehovah Raffa, Elohim, Adonai, Jehovah, El Ohim, Jehovah Jireh, Jehovah Sabaoth, El Shaddai, Jehovah Nissi." I cannot remember the rest. It was as simple as one, two, three. We realized with clarity that the finger was the actual finger of God and that He was writing His very own names into the wall. The letters were shimmering in fiery gold, as if alive. We squinted to make out the names and suddenly realized that the signature in Hebrew was indeed alive.

The producer and I fell as if prostrate before the holiness of God's presence. What in the world did this all mean? A building marked for God? Hollywood being marked or doomed like King Belshazzar in the book of Daniel, whose days were numbered and found wanting? We both reflected upon these thoughts as the dream flowed into the second scene for me.

The Seven Trumpeters

My attention was then taken from the signatures of God. Dusk had settled over the valleys of Los Angeles like a deep, blue hazy blanket, given permission from the California sunset, ultimately announcing the evensong of birds and nature. The soft breeze that entices people to Southern California was cooling and felt refreshing to my face. It was my favorite time of day: dusk. I was alone in this scene and looked up at the top of the hotel from the street to see that angels had gathered and spread out atop the roof. There were seven angels standing along the roof of the hotel. Many artists have depicted angels from centuries of creative art, but these reminded me of the trumpeting angels at Christmas. Their bronzed faces were a combination of human and "out of this world" being, which is difficult to describe. They were incredible to look at. I can still see them in my mind as I write. Each was about twenty-five feet tall and dressed in gorgeous gold silk robes with magnificent sashes and tassels attached along the edges of the robes. Their giant golden wings fluttered in the cool breeze and seemed to be alive, like their bodies. The shiny golden trumpets were enormous, and the unison sound of herald was clearly heard over the entire city of Los Angeles, maybe even California, as the trumpeters blew their instruments. What was the heralding for, I wondered, and why were they standing atop this hotel?

The Lighthouse

In the circular drive leading up to the large brass doors of the Hilton, there is an opening in the roundabout that is beautifully landscaped, with a fountain that welcomes all motorists and visitors from around the world upon arrival. If you have attended an event here, the hurried doormen almost sweep one out of the passenger side and welcome a visitor like royalty to this entrance, while they tear off a parking number for identification. On this particular evening, however, a giant resplendent lighthouse replaced the fountain, and the light at the top shone throughout the city. I remember thinking how the black striped column and the glass top of the lighthouse dwarfed the hotel for all to see. What did this all mean, as I rolled over to finish the dream?

I awoke and immediately went into the bathroom so as to not awaken Paul, but to write everything down on a hotel pad. I remembered the clock read 3 a.m. on the cadenza as I shut the door. The time caught my attention and intrigued me again. What is it about this time frame and my visions, Lord?

At breakfast the next morning, I excitedly told Denny about his special hotel. As I recounted the dream to him, his face turned a little ashen in our famous circular booth flanked by pink and white striped fabric. He pulled out his leather wallet from the inner pocket of his suit jacket and unfolded a small scrap of paper that looked as if he had folded and refolded it hundreds of times. It was almost in shreds as he showed Paul and me how he carried the names of God with him everywhere he went. He was ecstatic and seemed validated by it all. He shared that he had buried four Bibles at the four corners outside of the hotel: north, south, east, and west. He and many Christian prayer warriors had walked the hotel in prayer on many occasions with holy oil. I told you he was something quite special in the Kingdom. He said if I ever had something like this dream again, I was to call, no matter the time or place. I promised I would but made sure he meant what he said. I am fairly certain that a GM never sleeps well in his own hotel, with so many problems to juggle.

Paul, Denny, and I prayed on every floor that day and in front of several hundred rooms and VIP suites. Construction had begun, and he wanted it to be anointed for God in the newest renovation. Who knew what the history of some of the occupants had been? Colorful, among other things I could imagine. I would also say it was more of a saturated cleansing prayer session we had.

Evening came, and Denny left Paul and me to enjoy unwinding from the busy day at the pool under the palm trees. Again, there is nothing quite like Southern California weather on a lovely evening, as the breeze washes over one's face in the twilight. As I contemplated the right hand of God, His names, and the signatures, I thought how unbelievably awesome to witness something like this in a dream. Again, I pondered what God wanted us to understand about the details of this dream. Why His finger and His signatures of the awesome names in Hebrew, why seven trumpets, and why the lighthouse? I was still thinking of this as I fell sound asleep that evening in the cabana room by the pool.

The Time Travelers

I was in a deep sleep when, astonishingly, I had the very exact dream of the hotel from the night before. I was even surprised within the dream that I was once again with the Jewish producer, sitting out by the pool under the umbrella, discussing the subject of abortion and once again profoundly stunned by the finger that appeared on the wall in front of us. But tonight, the right hand and the forefinger appeared and wrote the names of God to the side of the Hebrew names from the night before; this time, the names were written in Aramaic next to the Hebrew. The fiery living finger of God inscribed His names deeply into the stucco wall. Once more, we squinted to see the shimmering golden signatures. I remember exclaiming how beautiful and fancy the letters were of each golden name. Hebrew and Aramaic were side by side. Together, we marveled at the sight and wondered why we were chosen to see such a thing.

The second scene took me to the front of the hotel again, where night was falling over the landscape. The seven angels were standing serenely atop the hotel, blowing their trumpets in unison. The lighthouse was now protruding out of the roof of the hotel and could be seen for hundreds of miles as the next scene unfolded in my dream.

The Points of Light

In what appeared to be hundreds of lights in the sky, I looked to the eastern sky as a formation of lights aligned in pairs of twos; each set was descending slowly out of the California sky. I thought for a moment that they were moving stars or orbs, until I suddenly realized that the lights were the headlights of aircraft stacked in landing patterns streaming into Los Angeles International Airport (LAX). I was wondering if a special event might be taking place to bring these travelers to the West Coast, or perhaps it was the mundane time period of unusually heavy inbound traffic coming into the city airport. As the jumbo jets were approaching, I could see the passenger windows on the right side of each plane. The small oval portholes of the planes were each filled with an expectant face.

I was observing the mountaintop; each face was laser focused. Each person could only see the Hilton Hotel, for it was now perched on the mountaintop and completely lit up by the lighthouse. From my viewpoint, I could see the entire scope of hundreds of miles of vast low plains surrounding Los Angeles and the one point of interest, the hotel, which sat atop the mountain. The Hilton was standing regally above a valley of small cookie cutter community homes neatly built in rows. There were thousands upon thousands of houses in the distance. The plane's occupants were wondering what spectacular event was going on in this place. I wondered too. The heralding angels stood out as the light produced from this massive edifice atop the mountain whirled around the dark city.

I was released from the dream and now wide awake. What in the world? Why the same dream on two consecutive days? I was gripped with how odd it was to have these identical dreams. What did it all mean? I grinned in the dark as I peered at the small clock on the cadenza and waited for my eyes to adjust to the small blue light highlighting the dials on the face. It read 3 a.m. This time, I did not hesitate to jump out of bed to call Denny and again went into the bathroom behind closed doors to relay all I had seen. Together, in hushed tones in the early hours of the morning, we marveled at the somewhat Apocalyptic revelation. We both offered up a prayer that God might one day reveal some answers to our long list of questions. What did it mean for Los Angeles? And what was God telling the city by putting His living signatures upon the mountaintop hotel?

I was drawn to these particular scriptures below and the story of Daniel after the two consecutive dreams. I was hoping to find a clue to what God might have wanted to tell me concerning the times in which we were living. "When the Lord finished speaking to Moses on Mount Sinai, he gave him the two tablets of the covenant law, the tablets of stone inscribed by the finger of God" (Exodus 31:18). Chapter 5 in the book of Daniel tells us about a similar experience:

> *Suddenly the fingers of a human hand appeared and wrote on the plaster of the wall, near the lampstand in the royal palace. The king watched the hand as it wrote. His face turned pale and he was so frightened that his legs became weak and his knees were knocking. The king summoned the enchanters, astrologers and diviners. Then he said to these wise men of Babylon, "Whoever*

reads this writing and tells me what it means
will be clothed in purple and have a gold chain
placed around his neck, and he will be made the
third highest ruler in the kingdom." (

Daniel 5:5–7)

To give a little background on Daniel and his interpretation of the writing on the wall, it is written that Daniel and three of his friends were young Israelite captives from the royal house of Judah who had been exiled from Jerusalem to Babylon under King Nebuchadnezzar. God had allowed this abduction to take place because Judah had disobeyed God's word regarding covenant keeping, the Sabbath, and idolatry. Daniel, Hananiah, Misshael, and Azariah were from royal and noble households in Jerusalem and had been chosen with official favor to be trained for three years in the king's service because of their aptitude, looks, and education. Scripture also says that God had given them knowledge, wisdom, and understanding in all kinds of literature and learning and that Daniel, himself, had been given the understanding of visions and dreams of all kinds. (I thought I needed a Daniel myself right now, in thinking about some of these visions and dreams). Anyway, King Nebuchadnezzar had a curious dream in his second year of reign and brought in all of his astrologers, magicians, and diviners to try and interpret this dream. None could find the correct answers to give the king what he wanted. The book of

Daniel is fascinating; you should read it yourself to get the enormous weight of responsibility and wisdom upon young Daniel's shoulders, his reaction, and his dream interpretation. If he correctly interpreted, it would not only save the king's entourage of magicians from a death sentence, but also his noble friends and himself. He charged King Belshazzar with arrogance against the Lord of heaven and desecrated the sacred vessels. He had praised idols and had not honored God in all of his ways. God sent the hand that wrote the message on the plaster of the wall in the royal palace:

> This is the inscription that was written: mene, mene, tekel, parsin. "Here is what these words mean: Mene: God has numbered the days of your reign and brought it to an end. Tekel: You have been weighed on the scales and found wanting. Peres: Your kingdom is divided and given to the Medes and Persians." Then at Belshazzar's command, Daniel was clothed in purple, a gold chain was placed around his neck, and he was proclaimed the third highest ruler in the kingdom.

> (Daniel 5:25–29)

People who have read these consecutive dreams have all asked what my thoughts are concerning the hotel, the handwriting, the trumpeters, the points of light, and the lighthouse. Truthfully, I have no idea, but like the days of Belshazzar, I believe it was a severe warning to

Hollywood and the world it entertains. God put many of His names on that hotel in Hebrew and Aramaic. He had staked out His property. Maybe it is the total lack of value and character given its reputation and glaring disregard for morality that Hollywood portrays. The industry, like Belshazzar, is found wanting. It has not honored God, is not at all humble, and has put itself up against the Lord of heaven.

Remember that God is the same yesterday, today, and forever. As in the times of the ancients, the handwriting exposed the idolaters and their worship of the vilest of all imaginations that humankind could conjure up. Much like today, I make the comparison of the vain imaginations of producers, directors, scriptwriters, and movie moguls who market a message of glorified violence, materialism, money, greed, sex, and drugs, and who have glamorized all this to the world through the lens of the camera. Have we fallen prey to the entertainment industry and its gratifying essence of the demented soul? Yes. A few of my thoughts on the components of the dream are below.

The Lighthouse

A lighthouse is a beacon that helps a ship or boat fix its location or position. It is used as a navigational tool to guide sailors in safety. I believe that one of the interpretations for this lighthouse in the dream symbolizes Jesus, the light of the world. He will one day stand above all on the mountaintop to beckon those in darkness to "come unto me." Remember to fix your eyes on Jesus, Who is the Savior and the light of this world.

The Trumpets

Historically, trumpets heralded grand events of magnitude. In the Old and New Testaments, the trumpet sound was a symbol of critical importance, which might be a clarion call for victory, a signal for war, or a sign of mass celebration. Most often, the job of blowing the shofar was given to the Levite priests. However, in the book of Revelation, the trumpeters are sounded to cue the commencement of Apocalyptic events for the last days after the seals are broken. They are used to herald world-changing events pointing to doom, calamity, and destruction.

Actually, I was shocked to reread my dream journal to discover that there were seven trumpets on top of the Beverly Hills Hotel those two nights. I had never thought about counting them again, but it startled me to read that there are also seven trumpets mentioned in Revelation. Were these dreams pointing to the signs of the times?

John, the writer of the revelations from God, was shown each trumpet vision, which will ultimately bring a new plague, destruction, or annihilation to civilization and planet earth. The seventh trumpet is reserved for the Day of the Lord, which will be Jesus's return. We should be ready for that day and not be taken by surprise, like the five foolish virgins in the story recorded in Matthew 25. If you remember the Great and Terrible Last Day in the first chapter of this book, God allowed me to hear a trumpet. Was it to be the seventh trumpet, as the sky opened up to reveal Jesus and His angels? I am astonished to this day to realize the importance of what He was revealing in these visions and dreams.

I pray that our nation will come to its senses and repent of her heinous sins, which strangle us as a people. We must unite to do this or fall off into the abyss with Satan's minions. Of course, I do pray for Hollywood and the entertainment industry it represents. I do pray that their hearts will be recalibrated to be living testimonies to the Almighty God. Now that would be the most miraculous move of God. I pray for the Christian believers who are in the creative arts and media. They are in need of our prayers and our support as they wade through the muck.

The Heart of the Matter

In the first scene, which included the hotel, the Jewish producer at the cabana pool addresses the most critical social and moral issue we currently face. I believe that one of the missions that Paul and I are called to today concerns defeating abortion while protecting the life of the preborn child. The legislation of infanticide is now egregious and will foreshadow the wrath of God upon this nation. Scripture clearly mandates that the calculated taking of life is murder and should be renounced at the state and national levels.

The children need us. They are vulnerable, at our mercy, and have no voice except ours to change this unfathomable and unthinkable act. What was it about Margaret Sanger and her Aryan philosophy that people cannot understand? She was the one responsible for founding an organization to annihilate the black community and those who were seen as physically, mentally, and socially challenged. When the moral authority of divine God is taken out of society, you will see secular morality take its place, which then is the demise of culture as we see it. It is an abomination unto the Lord for the killing fields of the womb and the complete diabolical scheme of the devil, who is evil. Those of us who are fighting on the front lines against this issue will never capitulate to the death warrants wielded by the abortionists and proponents of taking our children for convenience. We will fight to the end of time on this subject. The public should see the horrific effects of murdering the human family. The heinous taking of life and the nonchalance for which the international organization of Planned Parenthood has murdered hundreds of millions of our most vulnerable and voiceless citizens is almost unbearable, as the world stands by to allow such a holocaust of its children. How could the nations who witnessed the murders of millions of their children during the Holocaust of World War II allow such a thing to be legal? It is an oxymoron in thought, word, and unthinkable deed.

The discourse is silent except to those who find the idea so abhorrent and repugnant. The courts that do not stop this will be held accountable, the judges and lawyers who defy the value of life for political gain will be held accountable, and the physicians who have abdicated the Hippocratic oath and ethics of medicine in saving lives will be held accountable. The politicians and legislators who have promoted abortion as women's rights for votes will have blood on their hands, reproductive rights groups will be held accountable, and the public will be held accountable for silence while the babies scream in the womb. Get ready, world; the time is at hand. The trumpets are heralding in the new dimension. The handwriting on the wall is God's forewarning of what He is about to do. Woe to those who take this warning lightly.

The Time Travelers

As for the time travelers, I am not quite sure what they mean. I still think of them to this day, as I remember their faces peering through the portholes of the plane. They were being flown in by the planeloads and drawn to the light and mountaintop experience they wanted so desperately. I will remain expectant and excited to find out what they might have represented.

The Godly Character of Daniel

In closing this chapter, I reread the book of Daniel to take an in-depth look at the differences of the gods of Babylon and the God of Judah and how each civilization affected the lives of its people. I also wanted to revisit the greatness of young Daniel and how he conducted himself in a foreign land as a captive in exile. What made him so great in the eyes of God and of King Nebuchadnezzar? He was given such unprecedented honor and favor in high places of the king's palace after interpreting the dreams. Why? Because Daniel had an unwavering respect for God and the moral laws he adhered to. His reputation was stellar not only in the palace, but throughout the land, until jealous pride pushed some officials to entrapment. Daniel did not capitulate to the gods of the world nor bow to worship them. Daniel absolutely amazes me. God could trust this young man with an entire nation; he was given unprecedented wisdom, knowledge, understanding, riches, leadership, high position, power, confidence, and reputation, and showed the ancient world at that time such miraculous deeds through his gift of interpretation and knowledge.

How about you? Can God trust you with an entire nation? King Nebuchadnezzar himself ultimately glorified God verbally. The example that God gives in His Word concerning Daniel is an excellent reminder that if we could all model and imitate this young man in our lives, we would be spiritual giants to live incredibly powerful and promoted lives in the natural world. I shall remain a watchman on the wall. Here I am, Lord. Use me.

Time to Reflect

1. What part of this vision came alive for you in a personal way? Why?
2. Does this vision create a sense of urgency for you to change something in the culture for the common good of everyone?

Scripture Study

1. Read John 9:1–7. How does Jesus contrast light and dark in relationship to His Kingdom work?
2. Read James 5:20. Can you impact the culture for the Kingdom?

Chapter 14

The Martyrs Come to Heaven

I saw thrones on which were seated those who had been given authority to judge. And I saw the souls of those who had been beheaded because of their testimony about Jesus and because of the word of God. They had not worshiped the beast or its image and had not received its mark on their foreheads or their hands. They came to life and reigned with Christ a thousand years. The rest of the dead did not come to life until the thousand years were ended. This is the first resurrection. Blessed and holy are those who share in the first resurrection. The second death has no power over them, but they will be priests of God and of Christ and will reign with him for a thousand years.

—Revelation 20:4–6

After the visions of the Fifth Seal and the Great and Terrible, I had the subject of the Christian martyrs on my heart in the deepest sense of emotional attachment. After rereading the above passage of scripture, I was haunted by the realization that the martyrs had given their lives for the Gospel; they sold out for the testimony of Jesus the Christ. I wondered how many it could possibly be. The Kingdom's heroes, who I call the hidden (maybe lost) department of God's soldiers, should be considered the truest elect from our past and present. We rarely speak of the martyrs and probably don't think of them too often. Guiltily, I must admit that I have not remembered them nor has my heart really ever been broken for them like it should. It was not until the vision of the Fifth Seal and the one you are about to read that I seriously gave these honored ones more than a passing thought. Only when media grasps a story of interest overseas do we think of these souls who courageously paved the way for the hundreds of millions who might have been eternally saved in our world because of their heroism. The whole concept is devastatingly true because of the enormous brutal sufferings and risks martyrs have endured throughout the ages. What a price they paid for us. We are told in scripture that many will have to endure these atrocities to usher in the Last Days, as valiant Christendom takes its eternal place in history. I am so grateful that the writers of scripture have included passages about how bravely and beautifully they will serve our God in the end.

Martyrdom does not live next door to most of us in

our lovely towers of safety and village towns of surplus, nor does it come knocking on the door of a suspecting victim. It is swift and savage to those who have been chosen for this. Terrorism has viciously wracked our age of innocence. I think of the unparalleled bravery and honor that is due our martyred warriors, both young and old. I want to encourage our world to care more for their heroic acts and never forget their memory. Thinking of the madmen in black, the terrorists of this present age remind me of the grotesque Orcs of Middle Earth, from J. R. R. Tolkien's *The Lord of the Rings*, who raged toward the annihilation of the good. They also remind me of the several passages in Revelation that talk about the black locust or the horsemen in black who come to destroy.

I think the most impressionable of my memories of modern-day martyrdom will be the unquestionable courage of the twenty-one Egyptian Coptic Christian "men in orange," kneeling somewhere on a beach in the Middle East, facing execution by beheading. Could I face the daunting realization that I was about to be murdered for simply being an orthodox Christian worker and follower of Jesus? It is a hard question to pose and to ultimately comprehend. Probably the most searing visual in my memory of that televised event will be the angelic look of strength and courage on each man's face as the executioner wielded his sharpened weapon. Such bravery before the onslaught of death surely could not be missed by the general public.

I can only imagine what they were praying to our Lord

in their heinous situation. It might have been something like this: "Father in heaven, be merciful to me, forgive me for my sins, keep watch over my beloved family until we meet again, and give me the power and strength of Your Holy Spirit to endure this death." What does one say at such a meeting with death? What goes through the mind of these fearless ones giving their life for the Gospel? Fear did not shadow the beautiful faces as I recall. Acts chapter 7 tells the powerful story of Stephan, who had a "face like that of an angel." He was the great New Testament ancient martyred after giving a thought-provoking and powerful sermon to the Sanhedrin (the elders and teachers of the Law), calling them stiff-necked and resistant to the work of the Holy Spirit while wholly rebellious to God. How does God handpick these saints? What supernatural gift of peace and calm must the Holy Spirit deliver at the end for a martyr to overcome this way of dying? I am humbled to even write this short paragraph describing my thoughts of them.

Likewise, I have heard firsthand of the courage of our own missionaries in India who embody this characteristic as they are beaten, raped, and burned alive for their faith. Their homes and villages are scorched to the ground just because they love Jesus and have been baptized into the faith. Yes, I cry out for the martyrs and wonder when God is going to avenge their death in the madness of a world gone crazy. Simply, a holocaust every day in the world of martyrdom. Surely, I believe there is a very special hell reserved for those diabolical killers who have taken the lives of our human family and harmed them so brutally.

Paul and I travel to mission fields abroad to minister and counsel Christian leaders who dedicate their lives in caring for the destitute and underserved; we see the Third World as it truly is: politically, socially, psychologically, and financially bankrupted by corruption. We have witnessed poverty; human traffickers; drug kings; worshippers of wooden, rock, and animal idols; human predators; and slumlords who are all stealing the very vibrancy of the nation. It has not been a pretty picture to witness the sickness of greed and the tainted hearts of power. Many of God's beloved people live on pennies a day, a handful of rice another day in these struggling countries. Yes, the subject of the martyrs has weighed heavily on my heart, and so I was genuinely surprised one afternoon that God allowed me a glimpse at how they will come to be known by all of us in heaven with the greatest and most due respect.

October 2014: St. Paul Westport: A Wooden Pew

It was an autumn afternoon in Connecticut; a little crisp but awash in the magnificent colors of fall. Our church sanctuary is uniquely designed with a grand gold Cross hanging from a vaulted, wooden ceiling centered over the altar. The beautiful Cross is draped with a simple, white silk cloth across its widespread bows. I was sitting in the third pew and could see the brilliant leaves from the trees in golden yellows, greens, browns, and reds, reflecting off the wood from the shafts of light peeking through the long windows. It was also the end of a day without any responsibility for me but to sit and quietly take in the last moments of a healing conference we were hosting that Saturday. A young evangelist from Florida, Michael Koulianos, was teaching on prayer alongside Paul and a Texas businessman, George Brandon. I've always loved studying voices, and Michael's can be mesmerizing when speaking about the pure image of Jesus. I was lost in deep thought about the same time he asked us to close our eyes and to "just enjoy the Lord and love on Him." It was a simple request for everyone at the close of our long day. After closing my eyes, I drifted away from the world in a peaceful little corner of the church pew. As I sat there quietly, the sanctuary was immediately transformed into a panoramic vision; I realized that God was opening up the vast heavens over our church roof for me to drink in the revelation of this epic event.

The Altar

Secretly, I've often had the urge to bust out in a waltz with Paul at our altar during a moving worship song; the thought is so tempting and inviting, until my reserved voice whispers, "The minister's wife will appear a little crazy." Waltzing also means I would have to be a ballroom dancer, to which I would answer that I am not. Despite all the black-tie events we've attended over the years,

I've never felt secure in the arms of the dancing pastor. Ballroom dancing is on my bucket list, so I keep a coupon in my wallet just in case a lesson or two is advertised in town. However, Paul is a great ballroom dancer because his wise Southern mother knew young men needed cotillion classes to advance their careers.

Today was a little different, as I gazed at the altar area. Today, it was ablaze with a brilliant light so bright that the massive gold Cross and the white veil seemed to disappear into the vastness of the light. I was not surprised to peer up the few steps leading to the chancel area of the altar to see Paul, dressed in elegant black tails, waiting for me. He stretched out his hand to take mine. The buttons on the waistcoat had been exquisitely polished, and his white tie and shirt were starched and ironed for this special occasion. I looked down shyly in the pew where I sat to find myself in the most spectacular blue beaded chiffon ball gown. If you saw Lily James in the movie *Cinderella*, my gown was encrusted with thousands of blue beads and crystals and yards of soft blue fabric, which mirrored hers in the movie. My dancing shoes matched the color of the gown, and I felt like a regal queen as I slipped out into the aisle and up to Paul to start an elegant waltz in the front of the church.

The massive vaulted ceiling of the sanctuary opened up into heaven, and there in front of us were millions of other ballroom dancers. The men were all in their regal tuxes, and each woman was adorned with extraordinary and vibrant hues of color in their gowns. It was a breathtaking scene of incredible beauty, color, and energy in the heavenly realm. The musicians in the orchestra, bedecked in tux and tie, numbered in the thousands. The vast space of heaven was full of the music, magnificence, and dancing energy, as we swirled and waltzed to the majestic instrumental notes.

As I observed the incredible celebratory scene, I was stunned to see Jesus Himself dancing and celebrating, right in the middle of all the dancers, laughing and swaying to the music. His smile was radiant as we breathed in the air of the holy presence surrounding us. Every dancer was aware of Jesus and could see Him through the mass numbers of people in the heavenly. He did, however, stick out a little in the crowd in His crisp white robes.

Thrillingly equal to that particular scene, I glanced over to see the face of God beaming from the right side of the jubilant celebration. Ah. Such peace and such joy our Father had in watching His children so happy, vivacious, and at peace with one another. I actually felt the pride He had for us and that we were there with Him in His own home forever. It was a compelling scene of love and affection and creative movement.

The Pebbled Walk

Without fanfare or any sort of signal on the dance floor, the pace slowed among the throngs of dancers. I thought we might be changing the waltz when I realized we all were taking our places and bowing, regally bowing, as if to the ground. Our voluminous skirts swept the golden surface in formal curtsy. Who might be arriving? The air was filled with an excited chatter that we might be seeing the Royals. Who were they? There, there they were! Yes, the Royals were spotted and coming up. A hush came over the legions of participants. While standing front and center, Jesus was welcoming them by a pathway coming up to the edge of heaven. A dusty, rocky road was coming up into the heavenly atmosphere that seemed to be hundreds of miles long. The color of dust was such a startling contrast to the beautiful atmosphere in which we were waiting in anticipation.

And then they came into sight. The first, second, the third traveler; by the thousands, they started to file into heaven by way of this dusty road. There was room for us all in the vast space. The trail of martyrs took weeks to get into heaven, but once in, I could sense their collective relief that they were finally home. Their clothes were ragged, tattered, and ancient, almost like burlap. Each piece of clothing was torn and soaked with old bloodstains that resembled rust. I could barely make out designs on most of their shirts. Their hair was matted and faces covered with caked mud, dust, and grime. War. They had been walking for some time now, maybe years in a war. Actually, they looked like death and were forlorn, but their eyes were alive now that they had arrived and were with their God. The crowds were a mix of all ages, all nationalities, and all colors. The emotional cost they had tolerated through tragedy was almost too much for me to carry, although I must. They had died for us, been disgraced and deprived for us, were spat upon, hung, ripped by bayonet and bullet for us, slain as unborn, as babes, as toddlers, as teens, as young men and young women, dying for the salvation and plan God had ordained through all the ages. The heavenly ballroom erupted into the purest of love for them. We knew they were God's most prestigious and revered, who had been created and entrusted with the highest spiritual gift of martyrdom. We bowed to the ground and curtsied, as they were the true kings and queens of earth. They were here, and they were safe with us, the ballroom dancers of believers. Our heavenly family was now completed, with the tattered among us. We would not leave one another for eternity but celebrate eternally with the godhead, for all time, from everlasting to everlasting.

As the vision was ending, I asked God for one last thing. I did not hesitate with the request nor feel arrogant or embarrassed about asking this small but great thing. I was just wondering if He might fulfill my one wish (well, really, since He is omnipotent, He must have known that I was going to ask this question from the beginning of my vision). I reminded God that I had seen Him in my heavenly vision years before and had seen the beautiful Jesus many times in the visions and dreams He had given me. I knew His gentle and merciful voice as Shepherd, the Great Leader, and imagined all these years that Jesus was my friend, but I was so curious to know if God would allow me just once to see the Holy Spirit.

I waited with bated breath to see what the Father might answer. I mean, really, who was I to ask such a favor? But within five short seconds, a massive volcano appeared over the top of the entire epic scene in heaven: dancers, musicians, the martyrs, and Jesus. Above the heads of all, but not over the face of God, was the most incredible volcanic rock structure I had ever seen from a *National Geographic* tabletop book. The structure came up from the space of the grand ballroom and rose over our heads up to the massive atmospheric space above us. The deep crevices etched in the side of the volcanic rock appeared as if it had erupted for thousands of years, from the beginning of time. To my utter amazement, it erupted into a spectacular firework display over the opened heavenly scene, but no ash or lava rock spewed out to spill over the sides into the crags or onto the dance floor. It was just an incredible, unfathomable burst of atomic energy of fire that shot straight up into the unseen darkness above. The shards of black, red, fiery emerald green, and jasper shot up into the atmosphere of heaven. The fires erupted and danced. I couldn't believe God would show me such an amazing light show.

The Vision Lifted

I sat stunned in the wooden pew. *Wow,* was all I could silently mouth in slow motion to God. "Wow, wow, wow! You are awesome, God. Thank You for granting me this privileged permission. I think I should have asked earlier, but never thought about it until the martyrs came to heaven. Life would have been much easier to know the power behind the name of Holy Spirit. Well, of course, Holy Spirit God should be a volcano. What else could He be for this day? Thank You, thank You, thank You for showing me this, Father."

Certainly, I have written this revelatory vision for you to seriously contemplate and ponder over. I could never have left it out; it was that important. Are there really any words in the human language to describe the martyrs? Beautiful, sorrowful, but courageously marked for us by God's hand. My faith has been strengthened because of their testimony and the test of death that all have had to walk through for the world of believers to acknowledge and honor in the end. I cannot begin to relay the overwhelming amazement and humbleness in thought and word that God would allow me to glimpse the person of the Holy Spirit as a powder keg of *dunamis* (Greek for "dynamite). If only we all realized that this atomic power lives within us to do His good work and His service in the world and to know that we have nothing, absolutely nothing, to fear. I once again want to openly ask for forgiveness, that I have not given the honor and due respect to this very thing that lives within me. If this volcanic power raised Jesus from the dead, how much more do we have of Him after His ascension to do His work? Be encouraged, my dear friends, and participate in this free volcanic explosion to take the world for Christ Jesus.

My prayer today, as I finish this season of dreams and visions, is that you will have hope for your own faith to be renewed, encouraged, and strengthened. You must never, ever give up in finding out about the God we serve and who you are in Christ. The saints who have gone before us are written in the annals of time, the holy books of history, by Him and for us as the road map to salvation and eternal life, with the volcanic power to fulfill all of His purposes in life.

Prayer

"Forgive us, Lord, for we have looked the other way. Forgive us that we have not risen up like the sons and daughters of the King God to say, 'Enough.' Forgive us and have mercy upon our souls. We do not want the blood of the martyrs on our hands of indifference. Have mercy upon those who are suffering and have suffered so deeply. Our hearts have not broken for those who have paid such a heavy price in our historical past and those in the present. Break our hearts for these who have marked the way before us. They are to be honored and revered. We personally know about these events and are not holding our world leaders and organizations accountable for their abominable and deceptive ways. Forgive us, we pray, for the lack of understanding. Forgive us for not exercising Your mighty power that lives within us; we tried to do it all in our own strength and power. We lay these requests upon the altar and ask that You give us incredible revelation, peace, joy, calm, perseverance, and love to overcome life's issues, so that we may grow in stature and wisdom to take the world for Jesus and to fulfill every purpose that you have created us for. In Your majestic name, the sovereign God of Abraham, Isaac, and Jacob, we ask Your forgiveness and ask that our lives may shine for You in courage and strength. Amen."

Time to Reflect

1. Describe your thoughts about this vision of heaven.
2. Have you ever thought of the martyrs who have given their lives for the Gospel? What would you want to say to a martyr if you met one?

Scripture Study

1. Read Romans 11:8–13. How powerful is the Holy Spirit?
2. Read 1 Corinthians 2:2–5. How does the Holy Spirit demonstrate His power in your life?

Conclusion

The Spirit of God has made me; the breath of the Almighty gives me life.

(*Job 33:4*)

There are so many stirring emotions I have in finishing this book on the extraordinary way in which God changed my life. As a child, I had one dark, recurring dream, actually a nightmare, that terrorized me for years. There were only three elements to the nightmare: a black square box, a white ball inside the black box, and the music from Rod Serling's *Twilight Zone*. The white ball would bounce off the four sides of the black box like it was trapped, to the rhythmic and haunting dark melody, which played over and over and over, to the abyss of hell to drive me mad. I would wake up screaming and dripping with sweat when the end came. I really believe my soul and mind must have said, "Enough is enough," and consciously cut off dreaming for years.

First, I wish John Paul Jackson were alive today to

personally thank him and tell him all I have seen and heard over the years. I know he would have wanted to read this book. We met John Paul in New Hampshire through our mutual friend, Harald Bredesen, our pastor-at-large. He was known for his ministry of the supernatural in revelatory dreams and visions, and encouraged me after meeting him to dream big. He always insisted that dreams and revelatory visions were where God was going to meet me when it was time. During our initial conversation, I told him I just didn't dream, after the nightmare encountered during my youth. His solution to my husband, Paul, was to get a good mattress. Ha! How can I ever thank him enough for this advice and thank God in His timing that He would indeed give me new messages of color, sound, taste, and insight, starting in my forties. Although I would probably say I was late in coming to the party (of dreaming and visions), my motto would definitely stand today as "better late than never."

Over the years, I have been surprised, overwhelmed, and humbled by the great power of the Holy Spirit in the exciting journey as a follower of Jesus. I pray that you have been engaged and encouraged in learning more about what God might be saying to you through some of these messages and my story of struggle and empowerment. However, there are several details of the visions that I continue to ask God about. What might the two steel bands encircling the earth mean in chapter 10? Some might say initially it was the equator, but I sensed it was something deeper that was fortified with steel

222

around the earth's circumference. Who was the man who ran into the narthex of the ancient church to declare the Fifth Seal had been opened? Was he the Ancient of Days? Who were the time travelers flying into LAX, and what might the seven angels have been trumpeting over the city or over individuals in Hollywood at the time? Were we about to celebrate the great feast in chapter 14? I would love to hear what you think. My mailbox is always open for discussion.

Yes, I did ask for a specific sign with my name on it and got more than I ever bargained for. Without "Rivers Wanted," I might have struggled for years in ministry to find a place of health, peace, and cause, without asking for it. He had to set up the perfect storm to get my attention; obviously, God did that and much more. If you need a personal touch from the Father, ask for a sign. Be specific, and wait to see what He will do to grab your heart forever.

Yes, God gives us our Kingdom destiny and grooms us through our life's experiences to ready us for His specific service call. Initially, my heart was radically broken for young women and children while living in Japan and traveling Asia on business during the 1980s. It was while serving as an active liaison on several Navy ombudsman boards and working with recovering prostitutes in the slums of Tokyo that God called me to my destiny, without even realizing it. He was breaking my heart as I traveled through the red-light districts in Asian cities, observing the young children (both boys and girls) who were selling sex to predators. At the time, human trafficking and sex slavery were not terms that had been coined publicly, but whatever the term, it was a heinous, horrific business for both men and women to be involved in. I came to hate the trafficking business with a vengeance after subsequent travel in Europe and South America. Traffickers have no conscience.

But this is a different day for those who are battling evil on the front of social justice. Today, we can all fight the many faces of heinous abuse by raising awareness and getting into the fray whenever possible. I often quip that if I were younger, I would become a ruthless human rights attorney to take out traffickers, in order to give life to children affected by the sex trade and to take a stand against abortion in the courts and state legislature. It is an egregious holocaust. Someone, please do this for me if you are struggling with a career change. I am too old to take the law boards (some will say, "Go for it, anyway"), but I will support any young lawyer who has a heart for the issues I fight. My service to the Lord now has been in finding the issues that absolutely break God's heart. Never give up the quest to find your purpose. We are our brother's keeper, it says in scripture. We are not put here on earth in a vacuum, without purpose, but must strive to continue His work as His hands, His eyes, His feet, and His heart for humankind. Romans 14:7 says, "None of us lives to himself." As individuals, we are spiritually responsible to God for the other people in our lives: whether family, friend, congregation, nation, or cause. We are members of creation teaming up with other members to make that difference, while remembering that we will answer to God at the end of the times. What could have been more final and more sobering than the Great and Terrible Last Day? Could the world ever be unified in love and peace like the vision of the African beauty? Kingdom people do not err on the side of weakness or spiritual apathy. God is sufficient to meet all of our needs: your needs and mine. We can do this collectively and in unity. We can all stand together as good people to fight evil. If the good do not stand, who will?

So my closing is this. Life with God at the helm of your ship is a ride of a lifetime. Yes, dream big, as John Paul Jackson would say. What else is life with God, if not exciting, adventurous, and dramatic? Time is short. Do something today, even if it is just one small thing to change the world. Be a twenty-first-century world-changer with God.

There is a scripture that I have come to cherish through the years. It is a great testament to the faith from the book of Acts. St. Paul, the apostle, in one of his finest pulpit hours in Athens, says this:

> *The God who made the world and everything in it, is the Lord of heaven and earth and does not live in temples built by hands. And he is not served by human hands, as if he needed anything, because he himself gives all men life and breath and everything else. From one man he made every nation of men, that they should inhabit the*

whole earth; and he determined the times set for them and the exact places where they should live. God did this so that men would seek him and perhaps reach out for him, though he is not far from each of us. For in him we live and move and have our being. As for some of your own poets have said, "We are his offspring." Therefore since we are God's offspring, we should not think that the divine being is like gold or silver or stone—an image made by man's design and skill. In the past God overlooked such ignorance, but now he commands all people everywhere to repent. For he has set a day when he will judge the world with justice by the man he has appointed. He has given proof of this to all men by raising him from the dead.

(Acts 17:24–31)

Amen.

It is the peace that surpasses all human understanding that I leave with you, my friend. May you find it abundantly, and as Martin Luther, the Great Reformer, said, "If God were to come tomorrow, we should all plant a tree today." I believe I will plant this year, as soon as the snow melts.

August 15 2002

Was	Tara Hitner
Ed	Michael Fletcher Garmer
Hancock Dist	Bra Krapp
mirrors/glass	2-3 older man
Boardroom	older woman + glasses
Table	myself
Direct TV	younger asian woman
couches/leather chairs	

Dream w/in a dream
    1st scene —
In the boardroom a man giving a presentation
of man sitting behind him — making green
older woman became irate because of the
A chatter going on — on request —

2nd scene — of presentation room opens up
to the boardroom
make-up line called Direct TV — A
that it How could this name belong to such a
glamorous line of product —
So I put on this startling red lipstick —
clocked — I was embarrassed I was hot —R.

227

Appendix

*Unless you people see miraculous signs and
wonders, Jesus told him, you will never believe.*

—*John 4:48*

Yes, God communicates through dreams, visions,
and trances to speak to and through His people. We all
have a unique dream language, if we tap into the wisdom
and process with which God communicates through us.
Dreams can be conversational, directional, instructional,
prophetic, revelatory, or simply a supernatural
communication from a supernatural God.

I use five simple tips in dreaming: (1) Pray for peace
and calmness as you fall asleep. Ask the Holy Spirit to
reveal. (2) Keep a dream journal and pen next to your
bed. Write a summary: colors, elements, characters,
conversation, emotions felt, mode of transportation used,
where you are in the dream, the situation, and date it. (3)
Seek God's Word and His will in interpretation. (4) Seek

out wise counsel in objectivity when possible. (5) Pray over your dreams, and enjoy the ride.

There are hundreds of passages in scripture that talk about dreams, visions, and the signs God gave people. Below are a few that will get you started on your journey:

Selected Bible Passages on Dreams

1. 1 Kings 3:5. The Lord comes to King Solomon in a dream.
2. 1 Samuel 28:6. Saul inquired of the Lord, but the Lord did not answer him by dreams or Urim (a physical means of revelation used by the high priest) or prophets.
3. Daniel 1:17. God gave wisdom and knowledge to the four young exiles, and to Daniel, he gave understanding of visions and dreams of all kinds.
4. Daniel 2:1–49. Nebuchadnezzar's dream. Daniel saves the lives of the king's astrologers and diviners
5. Daniel 4:1–37. Nebuchadnezzar's fascinating dream predicting his future and loss of royal title.
6. Daniel 7:1–28. Daniel and the four beasts.
7. Deuteronomy 13:1–3. Admonition concerning dream interpreters. Do not follow false gods.
8. Genesis 20:3. Abimelech's warning from God.
9. Genesis 28:12. Jacob's dream at Bethel. God's promise.
10. Genesis 31:24. God's warning to Laban.

11. Genesis 40:1–23. Joseph interprets the Cupbearer and the Baker's dreams in prison.
12. Genesis 41:1–57. Pharaoh's dream concerning the drought.
13. Jeremiah 23:28. "Let the prophet who has a dream, tell his dream."
14. Job 33:15. God speaks through dreams, in deep sleep, in a vision of the night.
15. Joel 2:28. Women will prophesy.
16. Judges 7:13–15. A Midianite's dream saves Israel in battle.
17. Matthew 1:20. Joseph's dream regarding Mary, his betrothed.
18. Matthew 2:12. The Magi are warned about King Herod.
19. Matthew 2:13. Joseph's escape to Egypt.
20. Matthew 2:19. After Herod's death, Joseph returns to Israel.
21. Matthew 27:19. Pilate's wife defends Jesus.

Selected Bible Passages on Visions

1. Acts 10:17. Peter's vision of the white sheet and unholy animals.
2. Acts 10:3. Cornelius calls to Peter.
3. Acts 16:9–10. Paul's call to Macedonia.
4. Acts 9:10–12. Ananias and Saul.
5. Daniel 2:19. Daniel's vision to interpret Nebuchadnezzar's dream.

6. Daniel 8:15. Daniel's futuristic vision of the Time of Wrath.
7. Ezekiel 1:1. Ezekiel's vision of God by the Kebar River.
8. Ezekiel 12:22. A declaration of fulfillment.
9. Genesis 15:1. Abram's visitation.
10. Habakkuk 2:2–3. God's instruction on how to handle a revelation.
11. Hosea 12:10. Hosea's word from the Lord.
12. Isaiah 1:1. Isaiah sees Jerusalem and Judah.
13. Jeremiah 23:16. Instruction on lying prophets.
14. Joel 2:28–31. God's revelatory outpouring leading up to the Last Days.
15. Lamentations 2:9. The curse on the prophets.
16. Numbers 12:6. Moses's relationship with God.
17. Obadiah 1:1. The vision of Obadiah.
18. Proverbs 29:18. What does society do when there is no revelation?
19. Psalm 89:19. When God speaks to His faithful.
20. Revelation 9:17. The sixth angel sounds the trumpet.

About the Author

Rivers Teske, international speaker, human rights advocate for the unborn and children in life-threatening crisis. She is Founder and President of Hidden Choices, Inc., an organization that supports young women and children living in poverty and extreme vulnerability. It was while living and working in Asia during the 1980's and 1990's she was passionately moved to make a profound difference in the lives of young people, who were abandoned, hungry, prostituted or discarded as "the world's throwaways." Today, she builds collaborative relationships with organizations and individuals who are intentional 21st century world changers.

She believes significant change can be made in today's global community through social investing, education and creative human possibility, defined by purpose and love. She believes in supporting the ethical entrepreneurial spirit in giving a hand up to feed and clothe the broken, while building successful alternatives into poverty stricken areas which transform the lives of people.

Prior to founding Hidden Choices, Ms. Teske owned and operated a successful apparel and manufacturing private label business under her name in Asia. She served as a Military Ombudsman & Liaison to Navy personnel and families, spearheaded several Mother Teresa Slum Projects in Tokyo & the Pacific Fleet with Naval Officers Wives Boards and Clubs and serves on several boards today in compassionate outreach to the community.

A graduate of Baylor University Ms. Teske currently resides in Texas with her husband, The Reverend Paul Teske.

"This trio h air an t-saoghal ash mairidh cell agues gaol."

"The world may come to an end, but love and music will endure."

- A Gaelic Proverb

CPSIA information can be obtained
at www.ICGtesting.com
Printed in the USA
LVHW032257190122
708805LV00019B/208